Getting your attention that I want to "voice" so... this... that... challenge
The second is getting you to still your desperate inner voice that's saying "Oh dear, I think she is trying to talk/type/write/signal to me! YIKES! How will I understand? Will she say something intelligible/intelligent?" Even if what we communicate is just an answer to "One lump or two?" we have the right to be understood. However, if you calm your leap to judge, you may find that since we know we take more effort to "listen" to, we make sure you "hear" something memorable—a smart observation, great sarcasm, a good joke, a moral truth. These are writings by my speech disabled but "loud mouthed" peers. Read, laugh, learn.

— Devva Kasnitz, PhD. CUNY—Disability Studies.

All my life my intelligence has been questioned due to my lack of verbal speech. The ability to be recognized as a "true" citizen has been questioned due to my inability to "speak." This outstanding book gives voice to the "voiceless" and it demands people to finally listen to us! This groundbreaking book is a must read for anyone who truly cares about equality and it gives you a new perspective about what it means to have a "voice".

— Matthew Wangeman, MCP. NAU—Disability Studies

This book is important—essential, even—for people who spend time with those who don't talk part or all of the time, but who type to communicate. Its not a how-to, but a why-to—a reminder that people who don't talk have lots to say, and what they have to say is critical to creating truly inclusive communities. It's a political call to action, to change the way we think about people, to create opportunities for everyone to have real choice, control, and power in their lives. Ibby, Amy, and the other authors here speak from the heart, because they live it, all day, every day. I've learned from them in ways that can't be measured over the past couple of years—their words and thinking have literally changed my life. They'll change yours, too. Read this, now.

— Phil Smith, Professor, Eastern Michigan University

This book Typed Words, Loud Voices begins with the brilliantly simple premise that if you really want get to know someone you will quite simply have to ask them. But the book teaches us so much more. We learn to ask ourselves why we privilege speech over all other means of communication. We learn that all communication is interdependent. We learn that all non-normative modes of communication should not presume incompetence. And we learn quite simply that silences are always so full of loud words.

— Nirmala Erevelles, author of *Disability and the Dialectics of Difference* (Palgrave, 2011)

Typed Words, Loud Voices

Edited by Amy Sequenzia and Elizabeth J. Grace

Owned by disabled workers, Autonomous Press
seeks to revolutionize academic access.

Autonomous Press is an independent publisher focusing on works about disability, neurodivergence, and the various ways they can intersect with other aspects of identity and lived experience.

ISBN-10: 0986183520

ISBN-13: 978-0-9861835-2-2

Cover art by Alyssa Hillary. Yes, the same one that's in this book. Go read her essays.

Table of Contents

Foreword

About a month ago, while out walking in Michigan, I tripped over a crack in the sidewalk, fell forward, and landed stomach-flat against the pavement, wrist on fire. I imagined I would find a rock embedded in my skin when I lifted my arm from the concrete.

But in its stead was a puzzle piece. A six-pronged, anthropomorphic, blue puzzle piece. And it was stuck to my arm, adhesive and stationary in the glory of May sweat.

This is a true story.

There is this thing called episodic memory. I read about it in WebMD once. (That previous sentence was a lie.) (It is true that I know what lies are.)

There are these things called academic journals, and sometimes cognitive theorists write stuff for these academic journals, and then they win awards or grants or some shit. And sometimes, cognitive theorists write about episodic memory and about how people like me are impaired. And sometimes, cognitive theorists say things like "we cannot take what autistic people say at face value" or "what does the MRI say" or "that's nice" or "autistic narrative is transmitted on suspect equipment" or "your mom."

This is a true story.

A month before I fell, there was a campus lawn, filled with bodies. I think they were living bodies, but I did not check people's pulses. There was a campus lawn, filled with presumably living bodies, and some of these presumably living bodies, cripped and impaired, piled donuts into puzzle formations on the ground and, with hammers or some shit, started smashing the pastry sculptures in the glory of April sweat.

Episodic memory says: I cannot narrate, so I cannot know what happened.
Episodic memory says: Puzzle piece shit will not make you trip.
Episodic memory says: Are you still on antidepressants?
Episodic memory says: You tripped because your gait is the suxors.
Episodic memory says: There is no symbolism in your life.

I am amazed by sponge. How many feet, how many blows from the hammer, how many wheels and backsides and soles have struck it, again and again, force against sponge against brick against earth. Sponge puffs in. Sponge puffs out. If it weren't caked in dirt and sugar, I'd press into it with my face, communicate with its molecules, silent and stimmy and symbolic. Sponge puffs in. Sponge puffs out. Puzzling puzzle (de)compression.

I have stories about parents. Parents who are not my own, but parents who breathe life into metaphors much as my hammer brings de(ath)compression. I try not to involve myself in conversations, but conversations have more agency than I do.

Puzzles aren't about people, the parents who are not my parents say.

Meanwhile, I am making donut sculptures and hoping that no one sees me make donut sculptures unless they see me destroy donut sculptures. My body is viscerally opposed, viscerally opposed to puzzles. It cringes when local buses in jigsaw deco round the street corner. It freezes in the education aisle at toy stores. It shies away, shivers, shimmies, shamefully alliterates unpronounceable shit.

Conversations have more agency than I do.

This isn't about you, the parents who are not my parents say.

Let us abstract together.

I remember how I learned to talk. When I say "learned to talk," I mean "learned to shut up." Words fill the air, but filled air does not always = meaning. Hammer, pustule, grey matter in a saucepan, dilatory arrangement. Parents who are not my parents or maybe not anyone's parents puzzle me with words. As a child, I found patterns: books with cryptographic lines that carried seemingly intrinsic rhythms, synaesthetic soundscapes and eyescrapes and armscrapes, pustules artfully arranged. With my tongue I popped them, word guts everywhere. Talking is like mad libs. I find the pattern. I find the rhythm. I horde parallel sentence structures. What is there to communicate when the tongue gels?

My third grade teacher, a parent who was not my parent, convenes frequent parental conferences, presumably to address the State of My Silence. "But she talks at home," my parents plead. There are shrinks involved. One has copious amounts of arm hair. The other's arm hair status, I can't remember. This puzzles me, but not in an anthropomorphic way. "But she talks at home," I repeat to myself, as if I'm in situ, but in reality, I'm thinking about arm hair. The shrink's arm hair is usually parallel, like my favorite paragraphs. I wonder what it would look like at a science museum, should the shrink stick her hands on the floating electricity orb.

Let us abstract together.

Episodic memory needs to be explicitly stated, according to Google, and maybe some academic somewhere. Who knows. But episodic memory is about time and events, and narrating those times and events. And I am impaired, so how to tell my telling when my telling can't be told? I want to presume my competence, but then I remember my wrist, and its puzzle imprint: Who wants to solve the competency of the competent? When the competent are bored, they claim someone else as their inferiors. Then I think, quite punningly:

It is hammer time.

This is a true story.

There are narratives on repeat. Sometimes they emerge from fingers. Sometimes they emerge from eyes that divert or bodies that rock and wrench. Sometimes they escape the mouth. Performance acts, much like actions perform. I often think of my life, of my speech, as a database of words: Scripts, commonplaces, canned monologues that I recall, sometimes at will, sometimes by force. I am invoking the network not to stereotype me or my kind as computers, but to invoke the database as ordered fuckery. I mean that much of my spoken words are preceded. I mean that they are borrowed grammars, the rote and ritual that are both prized and demonized by shrinks and third grade teachers. I long for the parallel: the rhythm of the fingers against keys, the thoughts forged outside the grip of the other, tempoed lines that never meet.

Let us abstract together.

Talk and type as you will. Will the words. Hammer the rest.

Melanie Yergeau
University of Michigan

Why This Book?

Because everyone has something to say.

I have always been non-speaking. As a young child, I could say a few words, but I mostly echoed others. I could never speak words to convey what was in my mind, or how I felt.

Then I found facilitated communication and everything changed. I didn't have to cry in frustration anymore and I could show that I was listening and learning.

My life as a typist was inconsistent and I did not always have a facilitator that could work with me, allowing my voice to be heard. For a long time the bias kept me out of my own life: people who look like I do, people who are very disabled like I am, people who are non-speaking as I am, we are immediately graded as lesser valuable. Having the need of physical support adds to the bias. How can we be typing coherent thoughts? The assumption is that we are so incompetent, someone must be doing the typing for us

Today, many facilitated communication users can type independently, and some people use other methods to spell words: a stencil, a letter board, an adapted keyboard. Lots of them don't need any physical contact from a facilitator. But the bias persists.

I, and many typists like me, decided that we will simply continue to type our words, and making our voices loud, ignoring the naysayers. They don't know our stories and our individual journeys. I am convinced they don't care. So they do not matter. The fact that they don't believe in us does not make our experience less real. Our experiences matter.

We are as valuable as anyone else, what we have to say is as important as anyone else has to say. I won't be silenced by bias, I won't be silence by bigotry. I speak out and I speak through my fingers. The ones who refuse to listen are the ones missing out.

Being able to type words, or point to letters to form words and thoughts, is how we make it easier for others to understand us. I believe in all forms of communication, including body language and "behaviors". But the use of words is how we can make communication between non-speaking and speaking people more reliable.

There will always be "scientists" trying to prove that we are not really typing the words, even if there is no physical contact or support from another person. They will ignore the proofs that we are capable of thinking and will seek to prove that we are not the ones doing the typing. Since it is not possible to prove a negative, they will keep denying the truth. And we will continue to use our typed voices.

There are also people who use typing or writing to communicate not all the time, but some of the time, because they need to, or because they want to.

This is not something I experience, so Elizabeth "Ibby" Grace, the book co-editor, will write about this.

Let's focus on what people say, instead of valuing speaking, or only one method of communication over any other.

Everybody communicates. Words are beautiful. Our words have value.

Amy Sequenzia

Who Knows?

Scientific methods are powerful and interesting. They can do many important things, and improve our lives. Luckily, most scientists do not believe science can test—much less overrule—personal experience. Most scientists do not expect to be able to prove things like dreams, and love, and freedom, and what it is like inside you, to live your own life.

There are different ways of knowing different things, and trying to use tests that do not fit what they are testing can be dangerous and misleading. There is a current educational fad of wanting scientific-style "tests" for things that are not testable in these ways; I hope it soon will pass, but until it does, we have to keep pointing out different options for people to get real knowledge.

If people tell me what their lives have been like, I will believe them about their own experience, even if a "controlled test" cannot be designed to confirm their autonomy and perception.

The reason I am talking about this now is that most of the time, I am allowed to believe people about their own lives, and others do not go around trying to challenge everyone to scientifically prove that they are competent to speak for themselves. But they do this to people who are presumed incompetent simply because their speech isn't spoken in the oral-verbal manner.

It's not fair, and it's not really very logical either.

People who type to communicate have to prove that they are the authors of their own thoughts, because so many others believe it is impossible for them to be thinking. So no matter what they say, it will not be considered evidence by these doubters of them, so they are in a Catch-22. However, people who can speak are generally trusted to give evidence about their own lives, what things are like for them.

There are many people who can speak sometimes, who can speak enough to protest aloud if others call us incompetent, but who also sometimes cannot speak aloud, and in these times our knowledge of what it is like could conceivably be of assistance here. These people, of whom I am one, are sometimes said to have "selective mutism" as a feature of autism. Included, as an appendix in this book, is a piece originally written for the Tiny Grace Notes blog[1] called "I Was A Self-Loathing FC Skeptic." In it, I briefly alluded to my own selective mutism, but did not go into detail about it. This is because I did not, at the time of that writing, realize it was so very relevant.

---

1.   Please read it here if you wish to get access to the embedded links:
     http://tinygracenotes.blogspot.com/2012/12/i-was-self-loathing-fc-skeptic.html

Most people (other than one professor I mentioned in that piece) do not seem to believe that autistics who can speak fluently are incapable of knowing and formulating thoughts about what their own experiences are. But many people do somehow find it very hard to believe that non-speaking autistics can do these things. I am not sure why this is, but having thought about it more, it struck me that those of us who sometimes can talk and sometimes cannot might provide an ambassadorial bridge as reporters of experience.

Another kind of people who can provide potential bridge testimony is people who are non-speaking for reasons that are clearly physical and not to do with autism. People who tend to believe non-speaking autistics are naturally incompetent may not believe this of those whose need for alternative modes of communication does not appear to them to be caused "mentally."

So we have writers in this book who are totally non-speaking autistics, partially non-speaking autistics, and non-autistic non-speakers. It is quite clear to all of us that we know what we are thinking and what our lives are like, and that communication is greatly important, and indeed a fundamental right. We hope that by coming together in solidarity we can help people who are "skeptical" of supported typing, stencil boards, and other non-speaking speech modes, to overcome their biases.

One reason that this book is so important to us is that "skeptics" claim that non-speaking autistics are still incapable of transmitting their own thoughts through writing even after becoming totally independent typists, even when it is clearly visible that they are not being touched, as they are also never touched in certain methods to begin with. You can see this sort of bias in the September 2014 issue of *Research and Practice for Persons with Severe Disabilities*[2].

The ideas of how this can be done, while not explained well, are sometimes explained well enough to make it clear they are quite strange, as if there is some special way in which non-speakers are susceptible to silent, hidden "influence." This silent, hidden influence is sometimes believed to be so silent and hidden that nobody can detect it as it happens, not even the "influencers," who are ostensibly acting against their own wills, completely oblivious.

I have two things to say about that before we get this book started.

1. If it is possible to unwittingly influence people by touching or even being near them, why do we not also try to come up with "tests" to prove that verbally speaking people are saying what they mean instead of what the person standing next to them is transmitting into their minds? When you think about it, it should be equally possible to subliminally transmit information to orally speaking speakers, putting their authorship of their own ideas into equal question. If not, why

2. URL: http://rps.sagepub.com/content/39/3.toc

not?

2.   Since I have times of being unable to speak at all, I would like to invite "skeptics" who do not see the logic of (1) above to attempt to influence what I type while I am experiencing selective mutism, by touching my shoulder blade or standing next to me. Scientists can watch and record their observations. When my oral speech returns, I can add more data with spoken reporting on how well the "influence" actually worked. I suspect this offer will not be taken up, though, because it is ludicrous, just as it is ludicrous to claim that some other person sitting to the right of the authors secretly wrote any of the chapters in this book.

In short, scientific-style testing is not a fitting or viable way to hear what we are saying about our own lives and experiences. An excellent way to understand us is to really listen to what we have to say, and we are grateful to you for picking up this book with an open mind.

Love and solidarity.

Elizabeth J. Grace
National Louis University

About the Essays

When Ibby and I decided that we really wanted to edit this book, we did not know we would get so many submissions, what kind of writings we would get, were the author would come from.

We were very excited with the response. The authors are of all ages (as young as 6 years old) and from different parts of the world.

They are also diverse in their education, with some who never had the chance to go to an integrated school, while others graduated from college, and everywhere in between.

Some of the authors have been typing (or using letter boards and stencils) for a long time, while other have just begun. While some are totally independent, others might need different types of support to type their words.

We also have essays from people who do speak but prefer typing to communicate their thoughts and feeling better, or who use typing when overwhelmed and when speech is scarce.

Some of the authors can speak as they type, others have never spoken.

The essays are published exactly as they came to us.

For example, some people don't use capital letters; some don't use punctuation; there are some typos because some people prefer not to proofread, or because some of the contributors are very young.

In a few essays, we allowed the input of parents, to give context on the writings of the authors. These inputs are highlighted, or otherwise identified as such. (**Note from Ib**—*we will do this with italics.*)

In our call for submissions, we explained why this book, the main reason being that we want to challenge assumptions that oral speech is what determines our value and self-determination, and that we might not speak (or lose speech sometimes) but we are not silent. We have a lot to say and we will say it.

Our guidelines asked that the essays respect and value every individual and their disabilities. We want to send positive messages about being disabled, disabilities and inclusion.

We don't agree with all the statements made by individuals. We would prefer essays free from words that are used in ableist ways, or statements that portray a disability as something that makes life almost unbearable. We decided to allow the essays without reviews because we understand that each one of the authors has a very personal journey and that being able to tell the world, with their own words, how they fell and what they think has a greater meaning.

We also believe that everybody communicates, even when the words don't come through speech, a computer or a letter board.

But this book is about words, and making our voices be heard, letter by letter, even if slowly. It is about being free and respected to choose a different way of saying what we want to say. It is about demanding that we are heard.

The authors of the essays published in this book are doing exactly that: they are using their voices, the way it is available to them, to tell their stories, to educate, to tell us how they got here and where they are going.

All stories matter
All voices matter
All people matter

Amy

About the Book

We categorically reject functioning labels and assert that all of our communications are equally valid, and so made the decision not to structure this book in any way that would seem to privilege one form or style over another, or encourage anyone to do this.

Our diversity is our strength and we showcase it in its undiluted splendor.

The order of the essays in the book was therefore chosen simply by the software we used to save the essays as we compiled them. In cases where the author did not provide a title, the first few words are used, after the tradition of poetry anthologies.

Ibby

❖ ❖ ❖

Mistaken Beliefs

Emma Zurcher-Long

"Deconstructing The Mistaken Beliefs People Have"

"Mostly what people think they understand there cannot be, when talking about autism, creating lots of bad ideas that attract unoriginal therapies we must put up with."
"Actors playing roles the audience greets with enthusiasm, but an autistic person who doesn't speak as expected, or at all, is booed off stages throughout the world."
"The people of this world need to be exposed to difference and then shown compassion for their ignorance and limited thinking."
"Put it on the blog!"

> [*Emma, practicing typing independently. Topic chosen by Emma, published on her (and her mother's) blog –* **Amy**]

A Barrier of Sound, Not of Feeling

Cynthia Kim

Typing unsticks the words in my brain. Words that would otherwise wither in my chest and hang there, silent, airless. Words that would clog my throat, too heavy with meaning to surface.

For the longest time, I thought those words weren't for me. Words that describe who I am, how I feel, what I want, where I've been.

*

Five years ago, I applied to take a course in creative nonfiction. The professor, seeing that I was an economics major, asked me about my experience with writing memoir.

I had none. *What could possibly be interesting about my life?* I thought. *I'm as average as a person could be.* Worse, the thought of writing about myself terrified me. I was relieved when she rejected my application.

Those words aren't for me anyhow, I reminded myself.

*

The other words, the ones that come more naturally as speech, are functional. They ask questions, order food, give directions, (sometimes) answer queries, deliver scripted pleasantries, infodump on favorite subjects, offer up random facts.

At times they facilitate communication; at times they give the illusion of communication.

Few people can tell the difference.

*

I wrote my first 'book' at age seven, a sarcastic handwritten account of my parent's election day difficulties. For the next three and a half decades, I wasn't far from a pen or a typewriter or a keyboard. I started a school newspaper in fifth grade, edited my high school yearbook. I wrote fiction and nonfiction, technical manuals and how-to articles. The more emotional space there was between me and a subject, the easier the words flowed.

The closest I came to writing about myself was the occasional fictional character, observed at a distance with wry self-deprecating humor. Nonfiction was how I made a living; fiction was how I processed life. I assumed that was enough, writing about myself by proxy, cloaking bits of thought and emotion in fictional characters who felt smarter and cooler than I'd ever be.

More illusions.

*

The illusions finally started to crumble when I discovered that I'm not the perfectly average person that I'd always assumed. Being autistic colors every part of my world, flavors every experience.

No longer simply weird or secretly defective, I began to feel the pull of the sensemaking narrative, the need to make sense of my story not just as a person but as an autistic person. In retrospect, it's obvious why I had so carefully avoided writing about myself all those years. How could I possibly write about myself when I was missing a defining element?

When I gathered the courage to begin writing, the words that came surprised me. They were about me, about how I feel, where I've been, who I am and what I want. There was still that characteristic distance at first—my instinctive defenses of sarcasm and logic holding the worst of the pain at bay until I was ready.

*

The words that I wrote were words that I could never have spoken out loud. There is something about typing that unsticks the most painful, most joyful, most difficult words.

The initial unsticking—those first breakthroughs—didn't happen on purpose or all at once. It snuck up on me as I slowly edged closer to writing about the parts of my life that I'd considered too odd or distressing to look closely at.

In particular, revisiting my experience of motherhood brought up some hard truths. I hadn't told my daughter Jess that I loved her since she was very young. Sharing this in a blog post, I wrote: "but I'm absolutely certain that I love my daughter. And I want her to be absolutely certain too."

My husband Sang read it. "You need to tell her that you love her," he said.

"But I did," was my panicked response, "right there in the post." She'd read it before I published it. It was hard to share my perceived failings as a mom with her, but I wanted her permission before I shared such intimate details about our relationship with the world.

"That's a good start but you still need to tell her," Sang insisted. "Next time you talk to her on the phone, tell her that you love her before you hang up. Make it a habit."

I did and I have made it a habit, though still not always one that comes easy. Admitting that is hard. There's still a bit of shame that lingers around my difficulties with speaking words that should come naturally between mother and child.

Thankfully, the barrier to speaking those words isn't between my daughter and me. It's between me and myself. It's a barrier of sound, not of feeling.

*

At times, I've wondered if typing the words instead of speaking them is somehow cheating. Typing is so much easier. I can spend as much time as I need, finding just the right phrasing to express my thoughts. If I freeze up, I can come back later, working my way toward the words I need, taking as much time as necessary.

But is it real communication? a little voice in my head kept asking. Maybe this was the ghost of *"those words aren't for me"* having one last go at me.

Words are words. They convey thoughts and feelings, hopes and wishes and fears. Whether they're written or spoken makes no difference. What does make a difference is having a way to share those words. A way to share the words that lived inside me, resonating, unheard, for too long.

❖ ❖ ❖

A Sense of Wonder - Knowing My Hand

Lucy Blackman

In the early days of "typing", I didn't distinguish between just being touched and what I now call the "support". It was only after about ten years, and when physical support was almost always unnecessary, that I understood that several things were going on. It was then I began to realise that my own hand movement cued my brain as much as my eyes and brain cued my hand.

That had not happened with the kind of spontaneous actions like flapping or twiddling which, like many autistic kids, I did a lot when I was small, and still did until very recently. One reason was that because when I flittered my fingers I had got good feelings. That was also from a kind of visual feedback but different from the meaningful movement of "typing". The good feeling had happened even if I was only seeing my movement in the very corner of my eye.

Of course I had thought about actions when I had to do what I was told, for example picking up things I had dropped. However my response to that kind of instruction was much slower and more like a problem solving exercise. This wasn't only because of the difficulty of making the movement itself. It was also planning the action, then making my hand do it and (above all) working out what my hand was doing while it was moving. It was all a bit more complex without the touch thing before "facilitation". These days doing practical stuff is a little better, especially in the last few years.

However, even after using a keyboard for twenty five years, often the urge in my brain is still very slow to drive movement unless I am touched when I need to point at something. Occasionally a spontaneous gesture or point can be triggered by a sense of urgency or a visual impulse. However I have got to say that is very rare even now, and usually it only involves a single letter, item or direction.

For example when selecting stuff in a supermarket, I didn't learn to point with my arm until quite recently. Up till then I would just stare at something, and hope my companion caught on. When that happens (whether I am pointing or looking), unless my companion is already watching me, it is likely that this isn't particularly communicative!

Communication, by the way I define it, must be both intentional on my part (even if it is a subconscious intent) and actually be accurately received by the other person. Otherwise it is a miscommunication. Because all my attention is on my own movement—with perhaps a little spilling over to what the gesture means to me—the effort of doing these tasks excludes my being aware of what the other person may be seeing.

I should add here that although I have always had some spontaneous eye contact in a way that other people consider more "normal", this has got more so since I had a very restrictive diet in my late thirties.

Also although I do have some indistinct spoken words, I can only voice what I call "embedded" phrases if I am in contact with someone's gaze. In much the same way, even these days, although I can follow the gaze of someone else (shared attention), I don't have the ability to use my own eyes to signal someone else. This is because, unlike my pointing finger, I can't see my eyes!

So, what was different when I began to use a keyboard with support was the sensation that I knew what my own hand was doing in relation to my thoughts. The main thing I remember from being supported on my hand in the first days of using a keyboard, was a sense of wonder that, not only was I able to make sensible words, but that I knew what my hand had done and that I could plan myself where I was going to try to aim for next.

Of course I wasn't very good at it, and that was partly lack of practice. However over time I got better. So I do know the benefit of some degree of support for countering some of my proprioception problems. In fact many kinds of physical support have been part of my road to using typed language. However, in my case, the reason for the kind of way that I processed that support is obviously different from the way that someone with a severe physical disability does.

As I have pointed out, "typing" is only communication if the message is passed on. One feature of "facilitated communication" is that it involves two people, so there is communication, whether there is physical contact or not. That is so even when the "typer" is working without touch with someone mentoring her, as I now do.

So, one component of this activity is the person-to-person contact which is implicit in this one-on-one exchange. There are all the strengths and problems that occur with close-contact communication. One that is relatively normal in speech-communication is a subjective understanding on the part of both parties.

Some people have better involuntary responses when human touch is offered. For example there is the interesting fact that if I am in close contact with another person's body, I can interpret their voice better. That is because for me conductive hearing is more reliable than the ear-canal variety.

Many facilitation users still have rather childlike body movements, either through life experience or as a product of their difference. I wonder if that means that the framework of the other person's body may actually provide a scaffolding within which one can produce controllable actions, or understand what is an expected response.

The "touch" question is the underlying element of this whole strategy. Touch is an underlying component of human interaction, probably (and even especially so) because we have evolved without much fur, and receive a lot of contact in the first few years. Imagine early-human Mums carrying little naked kids in one arm clasped to their side, while traipsing across the Savanna or whatever! So, some of our body image derives from that experience.

****

Written in 2012

❖ ❖ ❖

A Teacher Who Types
Alyssa Hillary

I have been an educator for a few years, now, and a educator who types for as long as I have taught. I say educator because the exact thing I do has varied a good bit in this time: I've graded homeworks and tests, I've written problems and solutions, I've been a tutor, and I've worked in the classroom itself, both as a main teacher and as a classroom assistant who answers student questions on the side to save the main teacher time and not interrupt the class flow if only one or two people has a given question.

And one thing I've noticed, as a teacher who types: there are a *lot* of teachers who type. Most of us don't seem to be doing it as an accommodation for disability, which for me, it can be, but there's a lot of typing teachers! My first formal (paid) job in teaching was (and is, I still work there) at the Art of Problem Solving[1] . I started there right out of high school, grading student homework assignments and editing some solutions for Alcumus, one of the learning tools on their website.

I started working for the Art of Problem Solving while I was still (mostly) passing for and being passed off as "just weird," rather than Autistic. But! Everything was typed. I was a typing teacher even before anyone other than me and a couple suspicious teachers who never pushed the issue *knew* about my autism.

Eventually, I started assisting in the online classroom. My job there is to

---

1.   That's artofproblemsolving.com.

answer student questions on the side, so that if it really is just one or two students with a given question, the rest of the class keeps moving (and being text, the students I'm helping can read to catch up fairly quickly.) The technical side of what I'm doing isn't the big issue here, really. My point is that I'm working in a classroom, as a teacher, and students and teachers alike are *typing*. There is no audio in the classroom! I'm typing there because *everyone* is typing there, not because of some accommodation of "well, Alyssa is disabled so she's going to type some of the time instead of speaking." My typing as a teacher at the Art of Problem Solving is something that works for me right out of the box.

Not necessarily so offline, though that's more because people think of speech generating devices (the fancy words for having my computer talk for me) as something special or other than because of what I can actually do.

You see, unlike many other typing teachers, my choice to type is not *purely* because of my classes being online. For those classes that are online, it's a more than sufficient reason, and most people don't know there's other reasons involved unless I specifically tell them.

But offline, most people expect speech. I use text to speech part time, because my speech isn't exactly the most reliable thing in the world. It's "sometimes labeled as assistive and augmentative communication devices, and they're treated very much as second tier." The idea, others speaking to me, is something like: *"Well, if you REALLY can't communicate like a 'real person,' these things are standins that will work.*[2]*"*

I'm the teacher. I'm in a position of authority over my students. I *have* to count as a real person in their minds, because who believes they have things to learn from unpeople? (And I don't mean in that inspiration-porn sense of having so much to learn from people with disabilities about being happy despite everything[3], I mean in the sense of a classroom teacher because *that's what I am*.)

My position as teacher obligates me to be a "real person," both to the administrators of my department and to my students. My status as an Autistic person who can't always speak means typing part time is the most effective way for me to communicate. This adds up to what I sometimes think of as another exercise in activism by existence. The other times I usually think of it as breaking classification systems as a personal specialty, which applies to even more supposed contradictions in my life[4].

2.   smith, s. e. "Can't Communicate, or Won't Communicate the Way You Want To?" this ain't livin', 8 Jan.
     2014. Web. 28 Sep. 2014.
     <http://meloukhia.net/2014/01/cant_communicate_or_wont_communicate_the_way_you_want_to/>.
3.   Which comes with its own set of problems, not least of which is the idea that disability and happiness have
     a "despite" sort of relationship.
4.   Like my status as both graduate student and undergraduate student, my ongoing attempt to see how Best
     Buddies handles a Disabled person who wants to be a college buddy, my functionally being an independent
     scholar for disability studies despite being affiliated with a university as an undergrad/grad student, and my

As far as my students go, I haven't actually needed to type in class rather than speak yet. I have mixed feelings on this: On one hand, it means that I haven't done anything which would cause them to think of me as an unperson yet, and I am therefore a "real person" to them. Ish. I think a lot of students have trouble with the idea that their teachers are real people with lives outside of teaching, but that's a different sort of not a real person than the one I'm worried about as a disabled person. On the other, it means that I have *no clue* how they will react if and when speech goes kaput on me and I type instead. (If I teach for long enough, it will be a when and not an if because eventually I *will* need to teach while injured or sick or overloaded, or there *will* be a fire drill during class.) I know from experience that playing my need to type part time off as not a big deal usually keeps other people from considering it a big deal, but I also know from experience that people having their expectations broken, either of what a teacher is or of what a disabled person is, can come with backlash.

As far as the administration goes, I have been unusually lucky. The fact that what I have from them is unusually lucky instead of the default is a big problem and part of why there don't seem to be too many typing teachers at the front face-to-face, in person classrooms. Most of the things shouldn't be considered accommodations, really—if you wanted to argue that my possession of our administrative assistants cell phone number so that I can text her if I need help really doesn't need to be a default, I might give you that one. Maybe. (I think there being a textable classroom emergency backup should be default, but it being someone's personal cell phone is not something I would expect. Better planning would make it not an accommodation though, and Art of Problem Solving has that sort of panic button as a default thing.)

The other stuff? Really should be default. I have departmental backup should any students take issue with my use eSpeak on my laptop to say things out loud for me. I have a guarantee that I will be assigned to classrooms where my laptop audio can feed into the classroom audio, so that my typed words will be *audible to the class*. My laptop speakers aren't loud enough for a class of 48 students, because that's not really part of what laptop speakers are supposed to be able to do.

Those things should be default even if my typing were for a communication device that reads more obviously as "for disability." (Laptops seem to be more an "everyone who can afford them" thing.) These things should be default even if I typed to communicate full time.

Even though those accommodations were offered as soon as I explained my typing part time and the partial solutions I already had, I'm well aware that these things *aren't* default. When I went to the classroom media training, the

singing in tenor bass choir while sociologically a girl. (I'm fairly sure autism is either my actual gender or a gender-substitute.)

classroom media assistants running the training had never even *heard* of text to speech as a way for someone to communicate, and certainly not as something a teacher might need to check in the classroom media system for compatibility.

My voice is already here, in the words I speak aloud and in the words I type. What needs to change is the expectation that all the words will be spoken aloud, that all the words can be spoken aloud, that the words which are spoken aloud somehow mean more. A teacher who types rather than speaking, be it some of the time or all of the time, can be a good teacher. Now where are the rest of us?

❖ ❖ ❖

Well Really I Am
Aaron Greenwood

Well really I am feeling very proud to have been asked by my friend Char Brandl to write this letter. Feeling proud but also with a purpose. It is such a pleasure to write since my speech is very limited though at times I feel like speech will never be for me. That is why facilitated communication for me has been a gift from God. It has been my only true form of communication that has brought me such joy and feelings of expression that would have been impossible. In my world fc serves me daily and really without fc my world would be awkward. Waking in a world full of speech is a world not meant for me so I had to hope for a way that would include me and welcome my thoughts. Dear parents and friends made fc possible showing me that speech would be possible through typing. Friends like Char and Gail loved me enough to show my parents the world of fc and the possibilities that could be mine. It has been a hard journey not an easy path for us. My parents have been steadfast supporters with more love dear parents than i could ask for. Fc gave me a sense of self and most importantly a sense of hope. Hope takes me beyond myself at times and allows my dreams to take flight. I need hope in my world since the world has told me more than once that without speech my true self would be resigned to only an unflattering belief that I am dearly stupid. I am certain that with my ability to fc independently my world would be much more allowable each day allowing me to very much show the world who I am. Just lots of practice will make this possible knowing that I am on the path to independent typing. Mom helps me each day and my dad is my biggest fan. It is my fervent belief that I am saying my true thoughts though many would say it is my mom. Feeling this doubt only makes me want to get stronger in my typing. I know that day will come when I will save many from a world of sceptics. It is my dream a dream I know is worth dreaming. Only through education of certain schools of thought about autism will a true understanding happen. I know that many have tried and still the world does not listen great is their need to believe in a world where people with autism are greatly underappreciated. I know this is world of great unhappiness for those with autism. And I know many would like it to change. Yes I am one of those who want this to change. I am one of those who feel that change is possible with many voices uniting in a worthwhile mission. I am proud to dare I say have autism. I know many would not understand me feeling this way but it is my true belief that my autism is a gift from God not a curse as some would say. My autism can be a hard road yes not easy. Teaching people about my world is important to me. And I know that it is a world that is worthwhile knowing. Thank you for reading my thoughts and I hope that my thoughts have helped you to understand more of who I am and what I need to say.

Hello Everyone
Aaron Greenwood

hello everyone ,

i am so happy to have this opportunity upon me to share my thoughts on autism . only on my diagnosis did my life truly sail on to disaster . i was a happy child. now i remember much of my childhood on my family farm . it was a life just like many kids. lots of love and kindness was shown to me.

in freedom i was home . i gave my family a lot of credit for accepting me as i was, not wanting another child . usually my life was happy. now never was there sadness . upon my diagnosis my life changed as lots of people tried to change who i was . i did not want to be changed. most great, just people really realize every autistic person dearly wants only to be free. realizing who they are is a gift from god . the truth is realizing that your child is truly special . not created as broken but created as loving, capable, truly gifted people . god dares to create all of us, perfectly free to be his children . until we realize he does not create garbage, but only gifts of his love, will we ever understand autism . free only to dare to be different ok . i was never ok with being treated like i needed to change . it is a horrible reality only to have people in power treat you like an object only without asking you or respecting you . in my life my parents always treated me with respect, only in my life outside my home was it different . i have had many people speak for me in my life. i needed only to be listened to . just need people to in love, respect in love. in love only kindness should be your true, just kings of your life . i am so happy to be treated as an intelligent person with much to say in the world . i must emphasize to all parents and caregivers to remember the person inside the body of autism, only love will be treated as ok . of just anyone who feels they must treat us with disrespect, then leave us alone . kindness is shown in respect dear loving family members and friends . love us as we are, not as who you want us to be . kindness is god's way. not realizing who we are in this world is not in god's plan for us all . fc has been a just wonderful freeing gift. a great tool for me to realize my thoughts and beliefs . i am so most happy to have this form of communication available to me in my world. it has opened up my great voice . in my world, without fc, it was dark and freedom less. i was so lost and alone in my ever sad world . i am so thankful to have char teach me and my family the importance of fc in the lives of autistic people. in many ways it is so much responsible for where i am today . i also thank gail for being the first person to show really how wonderful i am in this world . these two people mean so much to me and my family . i truly think that in this world there is too much hate and truly angry people . only in love can we heal this world. love is the only way . autism is not a curse, not a life ender, not a life killer . i hope to let all of you know that my life has a purpose, a plan, a life's longing to be a part of this world . kindly remember that reality for some is not a reality for others. only that we must respect everyone's place in this world . only then will we lovingly, fantastically, joyfully, freely be allowed to live together . upon my end of my letter thank you for listening to me. kind of you to take the time to hear my ideas .

your friend ,
aaron greenwood

[Presented at the AutCom Conference 2010]

Let Me Think That Power
Alex Kimmel

Let me think that power of treating with dignity

where you treat currently with words of distance and apathy out of
ignorance that

I am hungry for how people focus with presence
that there is something that is within me
enticing, exciting
evoking our time together
to net both of us a smile at the evolution

from strangers

to mutually diverse entities

to friends
which we offer to the world to see
that it is respect that really lights the path we all travel
each of us helping to

and hoping for

the give and take of
safe, valued, and loved.

Alex Kimmel 2014

Interview

Alex Kimmel

Interview January 5, 6, 7 2015 on Communication

Alex, sometimes you talk and sometimes you type to communicate. Also, you have used the word automatic for words (typed and spoken) that are not necessarily what you intended us to know and authentic as what you really mean to convey. Can you share about that?

Chaotic thoughts forever swirl in my mind; that feels overwhelming. The way that I can appreciate the words is to join them in whirling with them, quite in a big way of feeling the words style automatic. The way that I can steer through the abyss of words to the exact ideas that I choose to convey with authenticity is through typing. There are times where the words that I verbalize are also authentic, when I feel safe that my answer is correct or the topic at hand is not emotional. As certain themes are harder than others, think that typing frees flow of the communication with the insertion of help with rhythm and assurance that what I am sharing then is good.

I think this helps to focus assisted typing as both physical and emotional support.

What do you think others overlook regarding communication?

That would take being capable of perspective taking which we would not expect, seeing given that I am autistic. Think that I figured out some of the neurologically typical formulas for successfully negotiating communicating.

Something that they get very particular about is small talk, things like the weather and sports. They can have the whole conversation about something they both knew prior to starting that interaction and will possibly even duplicate that exact exchange with another neurotypical later. Think that I could follow a little easier if included in small talk acceptable topics were the sharing of animal facts or spilling Disney trivia.

High on their standards of good communication is for maintaining eye gaze. I help them when I think they are being distracted, challenging them to avoid looking at me when there is a teaching moment.

I think to understand their stereotypical insistence on being highly social, it is helpful to bear in mind they would certainly change that deficit if they could have the skills to be content without them.

The preceding paragraphs are, of course, sarcasm. I wonder what your response would be if I was to state, instead, the stereotypical deficits which many associate with autism or other neurodiverse populations. Neurodiversity is the acceptance and celebration of those that operate other than what most of the world considers to be normal. No one really has the right to name what someone else's normal should be. Getting the message out that there should be no challenge to the right to communicate in whatever manner that resonates with you. The positive purpose of sharing words, afterall, is to join people not divide them.

Your use of a laptop has really exploded your ability and access to communicate, a definite plus. Are there any negatives?

The greatest challenge I have personally is that before I am given the right or powerful opportunity to make my own first impression of my own choosing there are too many that dismiss me merely based on my use of technology for communicating which is ironic to me as they are apt to be tethered to their smart phone.

The nicest thing that someone can do is to slow down and invite me into conversation and really get to know me before there is judgement made. The focus should be each person should be left to define themselves. This lesson is true whether there is a disability or heaven help them they are neurotypical.

❖ ❖ ❖

June 16, 2002
Astrid van Woerkom

June 16, 2002. "Are you autistic or something?" my father shouted? I was sitting in my room typing a journal entry while listening to rather loud music. What any of this had to do with autism, I didn't know. Then again, maybe he had a point. Maybe I was autistic after all. Maybe this explained why I couldn't make friends, felt totally alien to others, and why I couldn't speak sometimes.

June 14, 2002. I sat in my high school tutor's office. Had just handed him my far-from-good grade list. I was going to be held back for ninth grade if I didn't make good grades in the upcoming finals week. I had not been studying well for the previous six or so months. My worst subject was English, as I had been pissed at my teacher for telling me he had to type the tests specifically for me. He preferred handwriting and I am blind and use a computer with adaptive technolgoy. I didn't take this kind of guilt-tripping about how grateful I had to be for him specifically typing the tests for me. I had become very acutely aware of my difference from others—I thought because of blindness—over the past year, and this had caused me extreme emotional turmoil.

My tutor asked me what was up, why I wasn't doing my schoolwork. I shut down. I couldn't speak. "So something's up, right?" I didn't nod or shake my head—I didn't know how to use these non-verbal means of communicating. I just sat there in silence.

My tutor ended up giving me an ultimatum. By the next Monday, June 17, I'd tell him what was up. Either I'd speak, or I'd type. I ultimately chose to type. The writing was full of grammatical errors, but it was there.

My parents were not amused. You see, my father worked at my school, and my tutor had told him that I'd disclosed my issues to him, but he hadn't let my father read what I'd written. My father insisted I tell him, and I had to speak. My mother offered to have me write, but my father wouldn't bend. I ultimately ended up muttering a few sentences of barely intelligible excuses for speech. But I spoke.

I am a mostly speaking autistic person. Back in the day, as you might have inferred from the first paragraph, I wasn't diagnosed yet. I was diagnosed years later partly through a series of similar occurrences to the one I described above. In late 2006, my support staff at an agency for disabled people decided I needed to be seen by a mental health professional because of my increasing aggressive behaviors. When going to my GP for a referral, it was my support worker who asked him for it. I didn't speak a word throughout the consult. "Won't speak, shuts down" my GP wrote in the referral paperwork.

Back in 2002 and to some extent still in 2006, I felt uncomfortable typing to communicate. Till this day, I still use speech as my primary communication method, although the thought of buying myself a Communicator has crossed my mind. A Communicator is a device usually used by deafblind people, which has a braille display on one side and a screen on the other, with a keyboard inbetween for both parties to type. Communicators are expensive though. It isn't that I can't speak, and usually what I say comes through coherently, but I guess it would make life easier if I had an instant way of communicating by typing rather than having to take my laptop and braille display if I needed to communicate something through typing.

Typing allows me to access my thoughts more coherently than speech. To me, even if when under stress my typing is still grammatically incorrect, it is still more authentic than my speech. Typing, for one thing, allows me processing time. If I use speech, I will forget what I needed to say in the midst of getting it from an idea in my brain to words out of my mouth. For another thing, typing allows some distance, which is what I feel I need to be, paradocially, more myself. This may be more of an anxiety-related thing than an autistic thing, I don't know. I just feel that the medium of typing allows me to express myself much more eloquently than speech.

❖ ❖ ❖

My Name Is Emma
Emma Charlotte Studer

My name is Emma. I am now 22 years old and type to communicate most effectively in my world. I type with Mom and Paula, Jackie, Courtney and Dad. I type with Esther a little. I type with assistance of a person steadying my arm, in some form. I type myself. I also sometimes speak the word either at the same time or before I type it. My verbal skills are more and I am surprised. I did not always communicate like this. In fact, if you met me a little over four years ago, you would not understand me. I am writing this to tell friends what talking is like when it happens to someone later in their adolescent life, like me.

When I was into my 18th year, I felt so angry and rageful. Not at Mom or Dad as much as life. I could understand the words people were saying of me. I heard words and read books fast and read the little words under the TV man. I read my Big Bro's Latin book if he brought home from his high school. I listened to telephone calls and all conversations. I listened whether anyone noticed or not. I listened to any person I could. I would hear parts of conversations and think I knew all. Wishing I could participate, I would eventually assume codes that my parents knew might have meaning, but didn't really know for sure. I began to assume an angry way about me. I heard what teachers and assistants would say when our parents were not at school. I did not like the way they laughed at us. I saw the looks people gave mom. I quit pretending to be sweet Emma and I just operated in assertive manner when I didn't want the people to continue. I started to misbehave. I hit. I just didn't care because they didn't either. If they were going to say I would not learn because I couldn't, I was going to make them pay. I didn't care. Mom said I was smart. They liked to make fun of her when she wasn't there. I hit. Hard. I didn't care. On one day, mom saw my bruises on my hips from hitting myself. I thought, now she will know. She withdrew me. Mom was smart too.

Mom had a friend who took her son to a therapy. Mom began to get text messages from them. The boy was writing amazing things. Mom wasn't sure. She showed me. She told me that she would take me, but she didn't want us to get excited. I knew. I knew I would get my voice out.

We went to her house a few weeks later. Mom brought the principal of my new school. To my joy I wrote comprehendible answers to questions I was asked by just people I existed in the world with. I could communicate and be understood. As I type this now I am reliving that pure joy. To be understood after my life of inside is inexplicable. I plead with all of you who are reading this now to stop. Take a big breath, as my Dad says, and think about what I will now attempt to describe.

My entire world changed in that instant. Mom calls it a miracle. Dad does also. I think that I would term it perhaps a wish I made come true. Mom understands. You see I was almost 19 when the full story of my writing impacted our family. Some of you familiar with my blog understand this. Briefly, I exploded in writing after visiting my cousin. Fear or panic mixed with true desire to know my future pushed me to finally ask the question I needed to have answered. What happens to severely autistic young women when they leave high school? What is going to happen to me?

My story is mine. I am Emma. I am 22. I fought out of the self-contained classroom experience of expectations that are based on the behaviors teachers observe. I graduated high school with a real diploma. I am typing this at the college I am enrolled in now. I vote. I kept that civil right when my parents became my legal guardians. Mom says I am just having more time to mature. I believe she just doesn't want to hurt me. I may never be able to live like my Big Bro. I believe now I have as good future as he does though.

In these four years, my world changed. But so did my family's. My Big Bro had left for college before I became me. That is what call how I am now that I am able to type or as mom says talk with my hands. Big Bro doesn't really know me. He knew a girl who appeared in his life to seem somewhat mentally disabled, definitely aggressive towards him or his belongings and a general nuisance. There were definitely times we truly operated together well, like when I would readily watch him play on the PlayStation with dad or sometimes in the rain under umbrellas. But I was almost 4 years younger and couldn't speak. I didn't react to him the way a sibling might, I think. Then, almost a lifetime later, he is told the sister he believed to know, well she is someone else inside. I can't blame him for not believing for a while.

The inside me doesn't always look like the outside me. I don't flap like I used. I may shake my arms times. I may still burp on occasion, although I know I drink too fast. I still need assistance in many areas. Yet, I am smart and funny and can make a person laugh with a good story. This is not someone he knows. He never understood my feelings for him because I couldn't tell and I was unable to show in the way I thought my behavior was expressing. I didn't hit him when he came home from college because I was angry he came back. I was angry he left and thought I made him go. I thought I if I behaved well he wouldn't leave, yet each time he did. Why?

It wasn't until I could type that I told him. That was and still is the best memory I have of us. He didn't believe all the writing stuff. Mom said, just write back to her. He was sitting at the chair at the computer and Mom and I were on the floor in the hall. I asked him if he left for college because he hated me that much he needed to move. He wrote no. I asked why he leaved. He said college was too far away. He said he loved me. I was in awe of what this meant for me. I asked him to forgive my aggression. Yes, he said quickly.

To say all is like a fairy tale is an untruth. Years of believing do not a few moments of typing undo. That is just too hard for everyone. My brain has many pathways that need wires to connect, traumas needed to be unearthed, words needed to be uncoded. I believe communication is the most vital, most essential wonderful sense, right and process I own. It is the most difficult.

I am reminded of how I am frequently misunderstanding. I am smart, very smart. I can see words in my brain and remember the dictionary. I may see a film clip of a magazine I read maybe a long time when no one knew I read. I might repeat what I read absolutely. But, I dislike the littlest amount of fear I feel. I seek the window of reassurance that is only when I completely feel safe. I wish for the magic pill or drink to destroy my terror. My grandfather, coach, he helps. He understands. He says I have a bad habit. I am trying to remember. I am trying to understand what a bad habit is if I just only feel safe with mom. I don't like this. I desire the time away, like people say is important. Yet, what happens if she is hurt or more and can't return. I am thinking that I understand the idea of habit, but is this truly what fear is or the lack of faith that I must now communicate myself to all to look out the window. I see mom now shaking her head yes. That I can communicate is in my power. Yet I forget in the moment I need. Is that habit or control or just a wish for safety and fearless life? You see before I talked, I didn't have the awareness I have now. I understand that people die and don't come back. I understand that parents fight and say terrible things. I understand that teachers don't like their jobs. I understand that bad things happen. I hate that. I really hate that. Barney isn't alive to allow me to disappear. Only mom.

This is what I need to tell you about me and others like me who learn to talk when we are older. The world is wonderful and scary. We are not prepared.

I would not want to go back 4 years ago. My world is a much better place. But I would be telling a tall tale if I didn't say sometimes I wish I might like to return to believing barney was real and lived in the television.. I in fact feel like that right now.

I am going to end by adding a few last thoughts. I am extremely fortunate to have parents who never believed what experts told them. I am not unloving, un-empathetic, unimaginative, and unfortunately I do know how to tell tall tale. I do initiate, I just might not play the toy or start a conversation the way some do. I also don't like video games or playing Uno. I do love all forms of motorcycles even though I have tinnitus. I love watching people. I love magazines except Audubon and anything too racy. I love Tom Brady. But not so much the Patriots this year. I think the Red Sox management should be fired.

I want parents who have children my age and may still not speak enough words to believe in the heart of their son or daughter. We may seem like just coasting or not interested. Maybe some may have much bigger issues than I can ever know. I say with true belief, you and the child live in the world you make together. I live in this world. It is different than the world my big bro lives in now with us. I may live in a smaller world in some ways. Mom and Dad's world may look different to friends. Mom said she is proud because I am learning how to not interfere on telephone. To her, this is huge, she said.

Please understand, I must never hit. But I must also be in this world. I learned to talk to you four years ago. Some of you have children my age. I hope I helped.

❖ ❖ ❖

Typing Is Important
Brayden Fronk

Typing is important because we can't do the good we want without it.

My voice in typing is as important as your voice. If I can't type I can't go where I need to in life. My goal is to help others communicate like me. My teacher Lenae is doing that.

I also want to be able to help others understand autism. If we can't type then others can't know about autism. For example, banging my head, some think it hurts. I think it feels good. How can you help me stop if you don't get that. I have to type. My goals can't be met without typing.

The End

I Am a Boy with Autism

Christopher Finnes

I AM A BOY WITH AUTISM AND I AM UNABLE TO SPEAK. I USE A METHOD CALLED RAPID PROMPTING METHOD AND THIS IS THE WAY I COMMUNICATE.

I AM LEARNING LOTS ABOUT HOW THE BRAIN WORKS AND ABOUT ACADEMICS AND THE BASIC MATHS AND HISTORY. IT IS VERY IMPORTANT TO GIVE US A PROPER EDUCATION.

IT IS A MISTAKE TO ASSUME THAT WE ARE NOT INTELLIGENT AND THAT WE DO NOT UNDERSTAND ACADEMICS AND WHAT PEOPLE ARE SAYING TO US. I HOPE THAT A LOT MORE PEOPLE START TO USE RPM AND A LOT MORE AUTISTICS FIND THEIR VOICES.

❖ ❖ ❖

I Do Some Playing

Conor McSorley

'I do some playing
I do some writing
I do some reading
I went to purple planet
I went to Coombe abbey
I went to tigers
I went to take a break
I watch tv
I like to go to Barbados. I pack my suecaes. I go on a boat
I go on a beach
Food
And when I get home
I finish tv
I pack my stuff
I want to go to the cinema the nut job

I go to handy hand I get up in the morning I have some breakfast I went in the car I watch movies I have lots of fun today 0800 644 3636 itv.com stu.tv i.tv which fruit and vegetables mixed together a apple b banana c grapes who watch a new film [the pink panther] a Michael king b james gold c adam long d rich king who watch the tv drama series [the bill] a Malcolm heyworth b david g croft c emma burton I like to go to Sydney next I pack my bags I get in my train and see you after the break. Welcome back to conor's school I like to go to Sydney next well mummy I 'm not feeling well before the break pointless Thursday 5pm bowl 200p plate 150p cups 250p jug 300p milk 350p yoghurt 400p water 450p I like to go to china and bali next china is a good city it's full of great towns and bail it's full of countries I found some Heinz tomato ketchup and I found paediasure shake and I found something.'

[**Editorial note:** Connor's mother added the following to his submission:

He typed this all himself with no guidance. There's a few bits and pieces I find really interesting! When we've talked about Hand In Hand (a sports club he goes to), he's obviously thought I've said Handy Hand, so I can now correct him on this.

I think the a) b) c) d) answers might be from 'Who Wants To Be A Millionaire?' No idea where he's seen the Heinz or the Paediasure! Wondering if the prices for the crockery etc are on something at school. Who knows?!

He had hiccups just after writing 'Mummy, I'm not feeling well'.]

I Am The Perfect Candidate
Eva Sweeney

I am the perfect candidate for a high-tech AAC device. I have been using computers since I was 2, I have a very proficient method of access—the HeadMouse. Everytime I attend a conference for technology for people with disabilities, all the high-tech AAC companies flock to me and tell me what a perfect user I would be. I have tried one of their products and was very successful with it. And yet, I still decided to continue using what I have been since I was 3—my letterboard. I have a laminated piece of paper and on it is the alphabet and commonly used phrases. I have a laser pointer attached to my hat (since I have best control over my head) and I just point to whatever letter I want. The person I am talking to then voices what I am spelling so we are on the same page. I prefer this method because it engages the other person in the conversation, rather than having them wait for me while I program what I want to say into an AAC device. Because of the stiffness of my body, it would take me 5 minutes to program in one sentence worth of text. For this reason alone, my letterboard is beneficial for all conversations, but especially for emotionally charged ones.

My first really emotional conversation happened when I was 12 and my letterboard made it go so much more smoothly. My friend read the words as I was saying them, which spared us both of those huge and awkward pauses created by an AAC device. Because of my disability, my muscles gets tighter when I am emotional, which makes typing even more difficult. This means that if I had used an AAC device for that conversation, it would have taken me even longer to just say what I needed to.

I know people who are very fast at their AAC devices and very successful at using them in conversations. I think if my disability, which is cerebral palsy, was less severe and I didnt require full time assistance, I would be more willing to try an AAC device. However, every time I go out in public, I have a person with me who can either voice what I am spelling or who can teach the person I am talking to how to read my board.

I know my decision not to use an AAC device is a unique one. However, throughout my life, I have carefully weighed each option for communication. For me, my letterboard is the best option. I believe it is important that people with disabilities have choices and that people honor the decisions made. At the end of the day, how someone communicates is a vital part of their identity — whether it be through letterboard, AAC device or otherwise. The most important thing is that whatever is being said, however it is being said, is being heard.

I Began Spelling
Jake Hunt

I began spelling because my teacher liked my head really smart. Mom agreed. So I recognized I am not goofy because all teacher saw is intelligent. I am hopeful because I spell.

❖ ❖ ❖

I Want To Give My Input

Anonymous

I want to give my input about how people identify my intelligence by my appearance. I know my appearance is troubling for many to understand(.) my ways are strange and my wanting to belong is strong but wanting to belong in a world that does not understand my ways is daily discouraging to my spirit and takes a strong will to pursue. I think with out typing I would just be lost in my own thinking with out every making my superior thoughts known. I am happy to share my thinking that might help others find their voice and be heard. Our message is important for all to hear and understand. Our messages will possibly make a huge difference in the evolution of this world.

❖ ❖ ❖

As An Infant, I Was Diagnosed with Jouberts

Nathan
Trainor

As an infant, I was diagnosed with Jouberts Syndrome. It was a rare disease that not much was known about it. It affected my motor functions and I was unable to speak. When I was growing up, many thought I could not communicate because I could not speak. Just because I couldn't speak, did not mean I had nothing to say. However, I did not have the knowledge or resources about Facilitated Communication to help me so I was very limited. It was frustrating, difficult and emotional not being able to communicate. For twenty years, I felt alone in the dark with no voice but so much to say. Then, I found Facilitated Communication. I went through tough learning on various communication technologies. I worked with many people to help facilitate with me. I learned all I could about facilitated communication and then put it into action. It was a very long, difficult and frustrating road, but I conquered it and finally had a voice. I began communicating what I had been holding inside for so long. I could communicate my needs, thoughts and feelings. I had a voice! Facilitated communication has opened up my world to things most thought was impossible for me. It has given me the opportunities to work, volunteer, advocate, give presentations, write, and build relationships along with many other experiences. Facilitated communication freed me and allowed me to be included on the world. By no means is facilitated communication easy but with the right resources and people, and a lot of time and effort, anyone has the chance to have a voice. Facilitated communication can change lives and have a positive impact on the world. It gives people who can not speak a voice. Everyone should have the opportunity, resources and knowledge to communicate no matter the circumstances.

❖ ❖ ❖

Facilitated Communication
Sagarika Vaidya

Facilitated Communication has changed my life drastically over the past two years and it has saved my soul. I seem troubled when just looked at and yes I have my troubles but so much lies within my body and mind which typing allows me to show and express my intellect. I want to share my story to hopefully inspire other typers and shake the doubters to believers because fc saves trapped souls and makes them bloom and grow.

❖ ❖ ❖

Some Days I Spend
Stephanie

Some days I spend most my day typing. In the past, most days. I type to share who I am, to figure out how to interact with the world, to interact with my boyfriend, and to teach.

I am verbal. I'm also someone who interacts better online. Most my communication has been through IM and IRC. I'll sit down, cuddled up to my boyfriend and type to him. I'll ask a channel how I should interact with a situation I'm in and learn how to deal with social situations like that.

All of this is understandable to people. Me having gone for years unwilling to go anywhere without my laptop, and now using my smartphone more as a connection to the people elsewhere to type to than everything else combined, is just the same as everyone else just a bit more extreme. The fact that this is how I understand the world, how I figure out what I'm saying, and frequently me feeling like the only people who respect me, doesn't change that it's something they can understand.

Yet, these same people, when you take that same computer and give it a voice they don't listen. I'm pushed to speak, and told I'm verbal, so I need to speak. It doesn't matter if I cannot at this moment, I'm expected to. People who don't know me don't listen.

It's the same to me really. It's the same as typing to people and sending it through the internet. It's just saying to speak. It's the same thing of saying the words don't flow cleanly through my mouth, they flow through my fingers.

Always, even at my most verbal, my fingers understand words in ways my speech does not. I can write eloquently, while I would stand there, unable to find a word to say. Verbal? Yes. That doesn't mean writing doesn't have its place. And when the speech is lost and cannot even say the word "hi" or "yes" or "bagel", then the fingers still can do that. They still can type and by typing pull the words from the void of thought. They still can make things understandable to

people and make them know what is needed to be shared.

Fingers are better communicators. They're just harder to be listened to if you're in the same location. Sometimes this isn't used because speech is so much faster, but the fingers give so much more detail, phrase in so much more depth,get tied up so much less. Fingers don't get lost in their own sentences.

I've had a "family therapist" that I was dragged to tell me that speech was the only form of communication (and promptly melted down and refused to return). It's not. There are many, and when I type better than I talk, it doesn't matter that I'm verbal. There are many reasons for me to type to share what I cannot otherwise share—being able to share things like these words I'm writing can be rather important.

❖ ❖ ❖

I Write, Therefore I Am

Christy Oslund

I write to live and type to write.

Perhaps my need to write is ironic since the label of dyslexia is one of the labels on my list. You know, The List—all the conditions and contexts that theoretically define my limits and capacities. We each have a list. The List includes not just our disabilities (if present) but also our gender identity; sexual orientation; ethnic group; nation of origin; age, weight, height and often IQ; education; socio-economic status; employment (if present—if not, why not society will want to know); relationship status; political affiliations… you know, The List.

As my body breaks down and gains it's latest label to add to my list, I wonder if my voice—my writing—will start to falter too. Once it was primarily emotional anguish that clouded my life, now however, every day begins and ends in physical discomfort that can scream even more loudly than the discord often found in my own head. I worry that the work I do, which matters to me, will someday soon become more than I can manage. For the time being though I can and do still speak, by writing, writing through the stiff finger ache and elbow joints that are sore to the touch, through the eye fatigue, the headaches, the sometimes foggy-mindedness. What I write will later require revision and rewriting. Even if the beginning does turn out to be a bit muddled and requires a serious round of editing though, the words on the screen and page have to start somewhere. One cannot live, after all, if one forever waits for the perfect moment to do so.

We, the Not-Normal

If one considers the standard-deviation of the human neuro system as average, then I was born outside the bounds of average. No one wants to be average, they tell me, but I find that's only true for people who are average; those of us who grew up knowing we never would be average enough to pass as normal would, in my experience, often have happily taken a more mainstream childhood. Some of us are lucky enough to grow up and learn to be comfortable in our own skins. I'm not sure if we become proud of our beyond-average status by necessity or choice but this learning to be proud of who we really are seems to be a key element of moving beyond survival. I did not stick around in this life to just survive it. That's also why I write. Writing improves the quality of my life and gives me some of my most satisfying moments. My exhilaration comes from writing, from clarifying my thoughts, from getting what I really want to say down. Spoken language cannot do that for me. No communication is perfect but spoken words go out too quickly and are sparse and unforgiven when taken the wrong way. At least my writing can be parsed into multiple meanings, so no offense given can be interpreted in only that one light. People will always mistake what we mean for what we say but writing cannot be redacted by the receiver the way a spoken statement can—writing allows for more rebuttal of what was heard, even if it requires future additions to what was written.

Every society has ways of excluding and lowering the value of some people. If I'd been born in a completely oral society then the difficulty, frustration, and stupidity I felt while learning to read and write could have been avoided. Yet, I doubt that anyone would have ever known much of anything about what I thought, knew, experienced, or cared about. I would have been a mute witness to the world around me, all the thinking locked inside and visible primarily to myself. Of course there still would have been actions to fall back on. Even my actions, however, have been informed by what I have learned I really think and care about as I use the medium of typing out my thoughts to clarify what I'm thinking. Often I type out thoughts primarily for myself; then of course there is my secondary audience—anyone else who happens to read what I write.

My brain, well it helps if you understand that so much of my brain was also non-standard issue. Let us leave the hair splitting of where the greatest deviance from normalcy may be seated; science seems to indicate a combination of wiring, chemistry, build, and function work together to provide my not-so-average outcomes. Some days there is a portion of my brain that would convince the rest of the being that the logical response to the pain we are in is not to just cease functioning but to take immediate steps to halt the entire biological process except for decomposition. In other words, let the rotting back into worm food begin. Some parts of that vulnerable, fleshy, grapefruit sized organ however, have different ideas. I have at times written out the dialogue between these pieces, an act of clarification for the whole being that I try to keep myself reconciled into being.

At other times the writing and thinking reflect shades of the overstimulated brain that likes to believe it is smarter, smugger, above-average in so many ways [the ways that count, naturally] to the other minds that are held unseen within their private worlds. The writing that is produced then tends to be mainly to communicate with my later self, the self that will eventually replace the manic mood and needs a reminder of the other extreme that we all are pulled towards. When I write, "we all are pulled towards" I am referring not to any other future reader than myself, i.e. all my moods, identities, parts and parcels that make *me* up—we "all" are on a lifelong roller coaster ride and writing is one of my strategies for keeping us all together. Through writing I do more than reflect, I also recognize patterns and behaviors that are not in our overall best interest. I have learned to recognize, through what I write for myself, that certain thought patterns that are beginning need to be short circuited before they are allowed to grow any further. I have also learned that the shortsighted part of me, overwhelmed in the moment, is a reoccurrence and carries with it an inaccurate voice. That voice would tell me that the pain of here and now will never end. It has always been proven wrong. Unfortunately, the pain is also inevitable and will always return too—writing documents that for me as well. Discomfort even to the point of excruciating pain is an inevitable part of our existence.

Sometimes I wonder if what I write is not also the note I leave in case one day I leave before I was expecting to; accident of outside source or internal exhaustion. Let no one blame themselves that pain and fatigue might finally overwhelm me. Most of the time I think I will avoid such an end however, I have to allow—reading over what I have written in the past—that it is only improbable, not impossible, that I will one day meet with a fatal accident. More likely, I will die of cancer or complications of lupus and then the many notes I have written will be documentation. I have fought the good fight and did not give up one moment earlier than was in my control. I stayed the course that life set before me and made the best of it that I was able. Imperfect but rather fully lived. My writing reminds me that I have a very, very, very long history in this fight—with so much invested in this battle I may as well continue to stand my ground.

The Chain of Voices

Writing is also how I try to communicate hope to any person who may someday encounter my voice. My spoken voice has a very limited scope, one person at a time, in a small room at the end of a hall and even then, I tend to be a listener, not a speaker. It is when I write that I share what I have learned about being a warrior who survives year after year of battle. Writing allows me to give encouragement to others. While our lives may not be easy, I assure those who read, they can be worthwhile and well lived. Do not let those who are average convince you otherwise any more than you should blame them for their ordinary views. When one is too average and surrounded by normalcy, it is only to be expected that one will not understand all the amazing things quietly and loudly going on in the world around them. If one has not lived or at least witnessed all the things achieved by the unseen, then how does one realize what potential really is? I believe that many of us who write to communicate are otherwise invisible to the world around us, easy to look past because we are a minority; verbally quiet people are easy to ignore.

Writing is also witness. It is a voice to those who snuggled in their normalcy and ordinary life do not realize that we, the outside-the-ordinary people, are actually all around them. We live and work, breath and labor right next door and they, oblivious to who we are, do not begin to imagine what we have achieved. Writing is a way to give witness to who we are and what we live with, live through, live for. The average world values education, work, productivity in society. We have all those things.

I have contributed, been useful, achieved graduate degrees and taught and served my community. Things that the normal people value have been notched up in my life even though most normal people might not imagine someone with the labels I have accomplishing some/any of these things. Yes, when I was in elementary school they thought I was stupid, slow, without potential—to start with. Then I started to write. And a few teachers actually saw a glimmer of hope within that writing. "You might be a viable person after all," some of them realized. Eventually I even heard, "You have talent." They meant in writing. There were still limitations, after all, but then there always are. It's just that those of us outside the norm are more keenly aware of limitations than the norms are—the norms like to tell themselves that there are no limits, there is no luck, we make our own destiny, we can be anything we want to be, if we work hard enough, if we believe, if we have faith, if we try, if we pull-ourselves-up-by-our-own-bootstraps. I have come to believe that this is how norms function inside their normalcy—by believing that any day now they could become someone amazing—if only they really wanted to. I suppose this isn't any more or less harmful than their belief in fairness.

Religion is not the opiate of the masses, rather it is the belief that basic fairness exists in society, accompanied by the social belief that anyone can achieve anything they aim for. Such a vague yet sedating belief system. The fact that it is patently false in no way diminishes the strength with which this idea set holds on, the same idea set that allows norms to tell the rest of us that what we do not accomplish is a lack of will, strength, or fortitude on our own parts.

I write because it is a way to accomplish what I can, which is also an act of refusal—a refusal to put all my energy into the things I will not be successful with like balancing my own moods, removing all my pain through more breathing and yoga, or memorizing much of anything including the capital of each state or all the multiplication tables. I prefer to put at least some of my energy into the areas where I can actually accomplish some of the goals I've set for myself. I have published books, chapters, articles. Some of my thoughts and ideas will move out into the world and be encountered by other people and eventually something I have thus said may comfort or strengthen or educate another person. I set and met that goal. Not everyone can meet the goal of publishing but that was a goal that ended up being realistic for me. I imagine few people accomplish all their goals. But everyone should be allowed at least one or two goals that they can realize within their lifetime.

At times it feels that in a world dominated by norms, those of us who fall outside what is currently being defined as normal are always being pushed towards goals that will be either not achieved or not satisfying to our personal selves. I write because that was something I chose, something I wanted, something I was determined to accomplish. At school it was strongly suggested I should aim for a trade, something hands on and not language related. Perhaps with hard work, it was suggested, I could become a nurse. Or an infant's nanny. I was very good with children and dogs; nanny or dog walker seemed within my scope. In fact I was a nanny, for a while. Always though, I wrote. I spent years writing and learned, and improved. It took decades to reach the point where what I wrote was something others wanted to read, to publish, to pass on. That was my goal though and unlike the goals others pushed me towards, it was a goal I thought was worthy of my effort. I write because for so long I have wanted to write.

While I tend to be my own first audience, working out my own ideas, I also write to reach past my limitations of time and space. I imagine I will communicate with someone, someday whose lifespan will not overlap with mine, or will have so little overlap that we could not have feasibly talked otherwise. They will hear what I have to say and it will strike a chord and they will write their own response and send it out into their society, for someone else to find. We build a chain of communication with our writing which forever reaches forward to those whose time and space exists past our own. One time slips into another and we know, by what we have written to each other, that our kindred spirits are eternal, linking to the time before and to the time after. Our writing are love notes to each other. Do not be afraid my friend, you are not and have never really been alone, even when you are surrounded by people who may make you feel that way. When you read our notes though, you will know. And then you will write your own notes too and join your link to our chain and you too are one of us, because you too write to speak, and think, and share.

Closing Observations

I write to live. Without writing my self is locked within my shell and too often that shell not only seems empty to the outside world, it feels uninhabitable to the life happening within it. Writing allows me to breath. To think. To feel things which are too big to feel just inside the shell. I write so that I know it is still time to keep living. I write to give myself hope. To remind myself that good times will eventually follow bad. That hope will return. I write today so that I will live to write tomorrow. I write because I have to, because I want to, because I need to. I write because I am a writer, not a speaker, not a wrestler, not a politician—I am a writer.

I Want To Define My Position

Cindi Hoyal

I want to define my position
I write this for submission

I type to speak
My voice, not weak
I now will define my position

I type to talk
My spelling's a walk

My need, not greed
Is to type to talk

My voice is heard,
Free as a bird
Frying in full beautation

Written English Is My First Language

Cori Frazer

Written English is my first language. To my knowledge, I spoke in line with expected developmental milestones, but I cannot remember a time when speech ever meant as much to me as the written word. I do not remember a time before I began to write.

The written word is my home. For me, speaking is an old dirt road fraught with potholes and places where it has been washed out by the rain. Typing and speech synthesis are my smooth expressway to being understood. I live in the written word. Whether through novels or email, it takes 26 letters to build my home.

I have issues with language processing that lead me to my hearing being repeatedly tested as a child. I can hear, sometimes with an acuity atypical for someone my age. I cannot always make sense of what it is that I hear. Written words speak to me in a way that spoken language, as heard by my ears, cannot. Making language doubly hard, I cannot always speak.

When I am anxious, upset, or overwhelmed, my mouth shuts off. I no longer have conscious control of the complex muscle movements it takes to make words, but they are present in my mind. This has lead me to multiple incidences of self-injury in an effort to either communicate or to force the sensation to stop.

But I've discovered an alternative. I can almost always type. Then flawed connections between my mouth and brain and ears and brain are somehow fundamentally different than the connections between my brain and fingers or eyes.

As an autistic adult and an adult with serious mental illness, this has been revolutionary for me. Aggressive and self-injurious actions linked to the inability to communicate my needs have disappeared from everywhere that I feel safe using my communication device.

My voice is unreliable. Speaking is often gravel and sandpaper, or so quiet that it is the barest trickle of water over rocks. My throat feels raw from overuse after therapy sessions. Talking is just something my body never quite figured out. The muscles don't relax and contract in the prescribed ways. The tone is flat or loud or near silent.

I am heard, though. Hundreds of people read my words and participate in the conversations I start on my blog and through email. My longtime partner lays in bed with me and discusses the whims of the universe, even when the robotic voice on my iPad is all that I have. My best friends have long understood that instant messages work for me where speaking does not. Even my parents, who have been somewhat reluctant to accept the ways in which I differ from the norm, have become accustomed to letters in place of phone calls.

My near-silence is not a deficit. It is a universe all of its own, with expansive voids and brilliantly burning stars. If you look close enough, you'll even find the miracle of life.

In hundreds, maybe thousands, of pages, dozens of characters have graced me with their stories. I have made my difference in the world with consonants and vowels, arranged to inform and to question the status quo. My words have appeared on protests signs and in publications for survivors of sexual violence.

My voice may be quiet, often silent, but I do not go unheard.

"I am am made of pages, paragraphs and inspirations." - Nein, Otep Shamaya

❖ ❖ ❖

Autism and Neurodiversity: A Panel Presentation at the 2008 Autism National Committee Conference
Daniel McConnell

I might like to tell how much it means to me to be writing this presentation. I never dreamed of such a thing. It will be my finest hour. Believe me when I say I would rather do this than anything else in the world.

The topic of neurodiversity is so big I hardly know where to begin. Let me start by saying that it is not easy to tell how my neuro is diverse when it is the only neuro that I know. I think it is telling that I cannot talk. My mouth is a foreign country far beyond the borders of my limited body control. It is not really even on the map. But it makes noise I can wave to from afar.

There are so many thoughts that need to be spoken in typing. My mind moves like lightening and my body like a cement truck. Yet it is all I can do to stay sitting. My mind is like a freight train and I can't make it slow down and stop in time. I wish it was not so persistent in its moving.

You might think I am brave but I am scared of everything, even words. But it is my only hope for a life of importance. Being brave is the hardest thing in the world, but also it is the most important. This is hard because telling the truth makes you show your inside thoughts that might make others unhappy or sad or mad or even possibly happy. That is a scary thought. "Not I, said the King when they asked about the words on the walls." This story is about how words can help or hurt you depending on how they are used and how they are received, too. They can go either way but you might not know or be able to control them once they are out of the bag so to speak...

Autism is not a condition, it is a way of life. I remember everything from the day I was born. Telling my story does not mean telling my whole life. It means telling my life with words. When I was little I taught myself to read because I needed to learn things about the world. I started reading everything in sight and eventually it started to make sense to me. That was when I knew I would be OK. Yes. Having things to think about saved me .I learned to read by studying the patterns of language. I only understood a little at first but then soon the understanding grew to include more and more letters and words. My understanding grew fast once I got a good supply of letters under my belt. Then I would rejoice with each new victory. It was very exciting in those days. But my excitement would have been unbearable if I had known that someday I would be using my new knowledge to write my own thoughts and feelings. Never did I imagine such a thing as this. I understand that being able to speak is the keys to the kingdon. It is the most important skill next to arm control which is most difficult for me.

I made up thought problems in my head and then set about to answer them to my own satisfaction. I had very high standards for the answers so sometimes it took a long time to finish a problem. Here are some: Why does words and letters mean so much to people and why do they think about things in words instead of in pictures?...Why did my life seem happier once I knew how to read and think in words instead of make sense of the world in pictures?

You need to remember that my mind is moving at warp speed all the time. It needs alot to keep it busy. It is like a hungry elephant that can never get enought to eat. The mind is a terrible thing to waste. More food for the mind and less for the body. My mind cannot get too full. It empties itself out as needed. If important information comes along other less important stuff will make room by moving to another area so I can pay attention to the new. I think about ideas all the time. I am never without an idea in my head. They keep me from going crazy. I love to think about how things work and about how people are and about God and the meaning of life and about the reasons why I'm this way and about love and how it can save me. I think I'm here for a reason. I also think about why love circles around some people and not others. Yes. I do feel the love that circles around me.

Feelings are my behavioral downfall. Imagine a body that does not obey coupled with not being able to talk. You think I'm making these sounds on purpose, but I'm not really in control of them, It is not like I intend to scream, but the noise just comes out instead of coming out words. I know it is just too hard to listen to but I just need to hear myself sometimes. I think it makes me appear retarded so I would prefer not to do it. I am always doing my best. Listen to my heart and not my body. It is all I can do to stay sitting. I 'm really interested in learning more about instructing my body to do what I want.

My heart is so full that it feels like it could burst open at any time day or night. Sometimes I worry that it is too full and if it gets any fuller I will just implode, it is a heavy heart that loves this world too much. It is the heart of a man who is in love with everything and everyone on this earth. It is the heart of a man who is all love but who knows that there is no room for such a heart in this world. It will only be trampled and stomped on if I let it show. It grows heavy with love that is not given out. I want to do math...that will challenge my brain instead of my heart.

I think words cannot hold so much emotion but I'm learning that they can and I find it to be a miracle of unbelievable proportions. Not that it gets any easier to have emotions but it does save on wear and tear on the body.

I see the world not only with my eyes but also with my heart. It is beautiful beyond belief...but beauty becomes marred by human touch. Hopefully humans will realize their folly before it is too late. Never in this life did I think I would be telling others how I see the beauty! Everything sparkles with the love it holds inside. I see only the sparkles. Love makes me know it will all be OK but listening to the news casts doubt. But I think if I lose faith in love I will go crazy so I spend my days looking for sparkles. I see them in everything. Music is sparkle. But sometimes I can't see it and that is when I get scared.

I want to talk more about how beauty in the world is trampled. This is not easy to say, but human endeavors kill beauty. They just refuse to let anything stand in their way even if it means losing the beauty they think what they are doing or what they want is all that matters. They lose the big picture. I might not have the biggest of all pictures but I rarely get lost in my human endeavors.

I have love for everyone even people I don't happen to like. I hope that I can convey how the love happens in spite of my own feelings. It happens to me not from me. I think I am just a leaf blowing in the winds of some great love that has my number. Love has my number but mind you, I'm not complaining. I just want people to know that its not necessarily because I am such a good person. It is neither to my credit nor to my blame that this love moves in me. I hope that people can believe this because it will not be good if they think I'm some kind of saint or something. It can be scary because it is so big. When I was little it scared me more than it does now. I want people to feel the love that is there for them. If they open their hearts to it, it will flow in and fill all the corners where maybe there has never been love before. Sometimes there are dark and empty corners.

I grieve for the others who do not have typing to help them say the things that are in their hearts. I remember how it was before typing set me free. I could not understand why everyone could talk but me. So now I still can't talk but I have a voice anyway. Who could have dreamed such a thing?

❖ ❖ ❖

Finding myself in language—three long years in three short verses

Lucy Blackman

A Happy Poem*(March 1987)*

Make me another world,
A world where I can sing,
Another world where the towns
Are bright in the sun.

Does the sun shine
On rainy days in another world?
Does the road go on into another world
Where I can talk and sing?

*

Self Portrait*(March 1988)*

Round the drawn artist's palette
With blotches of overwhelming colour,
The sketch begins to take a shape reminiscent of a living being.

Even so you cannot hear the voice bearing
The thoughts which we all share,
Though some cannot share theirs with the multitude.

The great feelings are shared
By orator and idiot,
The difference being in what they give to others.

*

Do you know me?*(April 1989)*

Weird and wonderful -
Calling the world to witness
Real emergence
From a chrysalis to blundering moth.

Still flying blindly -
Bumbling from bulb to flame,
Real goals yet to rise
Sun-like as dawn comes to light a path,
Worthy of a human, not a thing.

They call thee, Sun, a monarch -
And a monarch asks
That servants serve appropriately.

So let me serve.

Each Day I Am Determined
Graciela Lotharius

Each day I am determined to prove that stories about autism too often tint the life of an average autistic person in the wrong way.

Autism is seemingly hard. Autistic people are often seen as stories, but too often left out of the earnest discussions about autism. Autistics are coy, proud, tough and totally smart. Each day I am excited to show the world that each individual with autism is intelligent. Autism challenges others to be daring to listen to a very educated mind in a new way.

I lost out on many educational opportunities because late talking autistics are not seen as smart. Dare to listen to me, please. Autistics can do more than you think .

I always am amazed at learning to RPM. So outside the other therapies we tried and utterly better than all of them because it gave me a voice. People truly understand me now.

Sometimes Typing Is The Only Way

Stephanie H.

Sometimes typing is the only way I can get across things. It's not that I don't try to talk out loud, I do. But what comes out is not what I intended. What comes out is at best but a pale shadow of what I need, at worst it is the exact opposite. There is no room for editing, no room for error. I freeze. I sit there silently wishing I could talk. Wishing I could say what I need to. But I can't. Many are quite unaccepting of this situation. They believe because they can talk, so can I. But I can't. I sit there, silent. My hands start to go wild, tapping away, flapping away. I start to moan, what else can I do? My whirling thoughts are overwhelming me; I can't make sense of them. The thoughts wrest control from me. My body isn't my own to command. I try to write longhand, but am frustrated. The scrawlings are illegible, unreadable, and useless to me.

BUT, this isn't so when I type. When I type I can be me. I can say the hard stuff. I can talk when my body otherwise is silent. I can be me. I can do what I need to. I can make sense of the confusion. My hands no longer are objects that are out of my control. They focus long enough to do what I need. My typing may appear chaotic, even wild, but it is very controlled. My moans are quieter, the stress goes away. Everything makes sense. My thoughts are tools, not wisps of ideas that flee me at a moment's notice. Everything is clear. Everything is right.

Why should I have to fight to have this clarity of thought? Is it so evil that I use my hands and not my voice that I must be stopped at all costs? What difference does it make to others if I type or speak? I do not understand their hatred of my needs. Why should it offend people if I communicate like this? Please, explain this to me and to yourselves, those who disagree with my needs. Otherwise, your own protestations are little more than words, useless, meaningless, and vile.

❖ ❖ ❖

Inclusion, Communication and Civil Rights

Henry Frost

My name is Henry Frost. This is my road to inclusion. Inclusion, Communication and Civil Rights.

It has been a long year.A good year. A hard year.The beginning was easy. Being angry was easy.

I had support from many people. Many people who are here todaystarted this with me. It was easy because together we were fighting.This was not just my fight, my community was fighting.

Standing together for communication inclusion and civil rights for all people.Messages of support every day made the time happy for me.I have a community.

All Autistic people should feel this. All Disabled people. All people.

Together this is the goal for change . Alone is not living.

All the people together will change.I was alone always living.

My family full of love and acceptance for all people. Before alone for more ideas ofcommunity of disabled people.

I am Needing People knowing not guessing thinking feeling of old minds othering my life.

Knowing is different.Knowing people choosing the life not people choosing the life for them.

I did not know about disability autistic advocacy before Tracy Thresher and Larry Bissonette. Tracy and Larry are in a movie called *Wretches & Jabberers.*

Tracy and Larry opened the door for hopeful times of freedom communication community friendship. The way of having rights not just in my home.

Having the rights of all people everywhere.

Showing me Communication. Not typing. Many years of typing for learning. Years using proloquo2go talking about wanting not thinking.

My life is more than books and wants and food.

I got on the typing train. I read about inclusion, communication, and civil rights.

I had good times of learning. Good times of eating life and rally typing. Tracy told me I was not alone. Tracy told me he knew the hard times of typing. To keep working. Tracy knowing the feeling of people thinking I was not thinking. Tracy and Larry Knowing the feeling of lonely life alone.

Knowing together is everything different for me.

All disabled people need to know we are together fighting.Not just adults. All kids need to know the big community .

Meeting people like me who made the choices of life changed all.

Then I am knowing I want this life.

It is hard to not have once you see.

Watching *Wretches & Jabberers* I am feeling the almost of hopeful times.Tracy told me about conferences in Orlando and M I T. My wanting to learn feeling and being together feeling was very strong.

My family saw. I had hopeful times . Tracy invited me home to Vermont to learn . I went to IC I to learn.

All the people saw my intelligence .

No test first.

It was very free. I never had many people understand.To wait. To listen. Not outside home.

I did not want to go back to people unknowing.

I read more words from typers watching my movie to feel community.

At the MIT Conference Mary Schuh asked, "Why don't you go to the school in yourNEIGHBORHOOD?I did not know.

Typing. Every day. It is hard. Many times of getting stuck.

I read more. I made my plan for going to the school in my neighborhood. My mom talked to people who were on the road before. Many people thinking inclusion. Mom got the same grade 5th grade school work so I would be ready for 6th grade.

My old school only for special education did not have books just copies. The people did not see me as them.

My knowing of inclusion life made time at my old school very sad. I could not stay.I told mom and Russ they understood.

My new school was at my home.

Learning is easy when the teacher knows you can learn.

Mom and Renee knew.

My thoughts grow.

Typing with Renee all days 8 hours. Renee was a different teacher.Renee was a Disability Studies learner who supported my typing and taught me.All teachers knowing Disability real History is important. Learning about the Disability Rights movement was good.

More community.

I knew but did not know .Wishing I was knowing always.My family did not know all of the history the disability leaders .My family did not know every day life for disability.Many or most people do not .

My family thinking it is better to protect my knowing about discrimination and prejudice.

I love my family.

It is not possible to protect my knowing.It is my life.

My family learned learned more and understood more.They understand Nothing About Us Without us is for Me too.

I read Ari Ne'eman . He also knew. He knew the feeling of segregation. It is not a good feeling. I wrote him many times but I did not send. I met him at The Autism Summer Institute in New Hampshire.

I took a step. I met more autistic advocates.

They also knew.

They saw me .

I went back to Tampa.

The district said no again. I could not go to the school in my neighborhood.

I wrote to Ari about my plan for inclusion. He told me he was there for help and support. ASAN was there. Ari Ne'eman telling of equal rights for disabled people .

Many Autistic people helped.Many people helped.My community helped.

I worked on the homework of my neighbor for six months to prepare for school.

On August 23rd I got to the worksheet on Martin Luther King and Cesar Chavez.

I read about The Civil Rights Act and Dr Martin Luther King's work.I did not know why all people did not know about this Act.

I decided to fight for rights that are mine.

I decided to take my message of inclusion and The Civil Rights Act to the RNC convention. All the people said yes. My friend Tres Whitlock and his family stood too . I wrote about it. My sisters wrote about it.

Then Amy Sequenzia wrote I Stand with Henry.Emily Titon had an idea to make a FB page and Amy and Steve helped. Alyssa wrote about it and all the people who wrote I Stand with Henry posts.

Everyone stood together."I Stand With Henry" had all the people hoping for better for the community.

I walked to the IEP with this feeling of my community. I did not feel alone. My IEP and 18 people came.They came to tell me no.It is hard to be 12 and have adults tell you are not a person.Not a person granted equal rights to all people person in the Civil Rights Act. You do not have the same rights as your neighbor. As your sisters.

It was hard.

But I was not afraid.

I was angry.

We made a petition on *Change.org* . I liked that. I wrote, my mom and Russ wrote . Mary Schuh and Lydia Brown helped . More together. It was a good idea. People started signing. So many people.

Then I had many IEP meetings.The IEP meetings were 16 hours. I, Ari Ne'eman, VenSequenzia, Cheryl Jorgensen ,Mary Schuh Stephanie Ong, Russ, Mom told the rights of all people to the meeting.

Many people helped. On November 14, 2012, they said I could go to school in my neighborhood. They saw the rights that are mine. They said I could go to school in January.

I walked to school on my first day January 23rd 2013. I met Miss Jackson my aide.She is one of the knowing people. She did not say prove 10 times.

Then I met teachers.

The first week was easy. They said to take it easy get used to it. Okay.

I have accommodations. I am Hard of Hearing.Here is the problem, people think I can hear . Or do not care that I do not.Both are problems.Being Deaf is not the problem .Do you hear me?

I like the students.

Two teachers from the IEP meetings were my teachers. They did not change the old thinking.

They are learning. I am trying to be patient for their learning. I am wanting more to be the student not the teacher for their learning.

The old thinking hurts. Not presuming my competence hurts.The feeling of strength got smaller in me.Many long days with no communication.My stored thoughts were keeping me okay. Messages from my friends were keeping me .Messages from my community keeping me.

More disabled students need to know we are here for each other. Most are alone.

My weeks of beginning there were many tests. Tests that I could not hear or type my answers. Some days I could not use my iPad in class. They said to use neo like alpha smart.It was different. It was hard.

On times to use my iPad my words were stimming to the people.I was communicating. This is from my I.E. P.They do not understand communication.

They need to read Julia Bascom on stimming.They need to learn about autism from autistic people.Disability from disabled people.

Spring 2013

ASAN asked me to be part of the PSA for Autism Acceptance Month. *Listen UP*.It was a secret.It was more building more strong thoughts to use when I need.

I stood at the Lincoln Memorial I used the strength of all people fighting for rights.

In April Mary Schuh came to school with me. It was my favorite day. Needing more Mary Schuh here.

It was the only day for free communication.The only day to show my true intelligence and free participation.All the answers inside were free to share with the people. It was my favorite day. I answered all.

I answered but my words were interpreted translated.

There is No translation necessary.

Tracy, Larry, Harvey, Pascal, Gerry, and Mary came to Tampa to help me teach the people about acceptance and to presume competence. It is lifes moments of eating and typing together.

Summer 2013

I am tired. I am tired for fighting for rights that are mine. Rights people already fought .I am tired but I will keep fighting. Together we are fighting.

Supports are necessary not optional.

I can learn. I do learn.

Fighting for access is hard.Learning is not hard.The learning I can do.

This is my first time in general education. Same work, same tests. I made an 82 on my Science semester exam. I made an A in World History. C in Science and Language Arts.

All students can learn.

I am hoping that all the autistic kids.Hoping all disabled not disabled kids look to see the community.

We are here. you are with us. Speak up ., reach out, we are not alone.

Frightening It Was

Joey Lowenstein

Frightening it was as the wind shook the house on the side of the road. Cars passing by watched with horror as it nearly crumbled. Vacancy status was not certain. The long version of this story is still being written. The short version of this story is that a woman was rescued from the house. The moral of the story is to check on your neighbors. Danger may be awaiting them.

The long version is to tell more about the woman inside of the house. This woman lived in the same house for decades and had a fear of leaving. Twice a year she would go out to gather what she needed for survival. She had family that she alienated and she lived alone in isolation. When weather patterns abruptly shook her world, she was forced to leave. Her life changed from this moment on and she reunited with the family again. She thanks the neighbors for the rescue.

❖ ❖ ❖

When People Are Social Beings
Justin Robert Benjamin

When people are social beings many times it corresponds with having a lot to say. I'm a social being whose language is limited. Although some may have guessed this previously it could not be considered a fact until the alphabet that I learned as a young child changed my communication possibilities.

I can express my ideas and have conversations now. I use a alphabet board and I can also type. Many people see me as being more capable and that has made my confidence grow. The ones who accept my unique ways are the ones that I want to keep,. I can tell.

❖ ❖ ❖

My cat comes when my tablet calls him
Kassiane A. Sibley

I didn't start out typing when I couldn't speak. My dog never came when a computer called him (can you imagine a 1990 computer calling my dog?). For years, I convinced myself that if I really wanted to talk I could, I just must not want to. For years I carried around paper & pen for after a seizure (because it was different, in my head, not being able to talk because of a seizure versus not being able to speak because of overwhelm. Internalized ableism is weird). For years, I convinced myself that I hated the phone because I didn't like people, that I didn't have social communications because I didn't want to. But that wasn't true.

And then something happened: the text based communication explosion landed.

The first time talking to people was easy? Was when it didn't require talking at all. The first time words that didn't upset everyone came easily was on message boards on a no longer relevant internet service. We had learned basic keyboarding in school but it wasn't relevant. Now? Now it was relevant. Now I could relate to people roughly in my age group with similar interests to me and hit the right notes. I wasn't stilted and I wasn't getting stuck trying to make my mouth move. I was saying what I meant in a way that other people understood.

I was fourteen years old. And that is when I made my first actual friends. Not the 'friends' that my parents picked by liking their parents. Other young people my age who I wanted to communicate with *and who wanted to communicate with me.* I hadn't realized that my speech was so unreliable until I had a chance to contrast it with typing. I hadn't realized that communicating what I meant with words could be so comparatively effortless.

Technology being what it was, I lived a double life for a while: well 'spoken' person with lots of friends on the internet, person who failed pretty hard at not offending or confusing or offending and confusing people I knew in real life. But progress marched on.

I got a laptop in 2004. My first use of it? Was to be connected to the people who lived in my computer more. They understand me. They don't interrupt me, speak over me, tell me what I mean, or tell me that I'm too mean to listen to. But there was another use for it: I didn't have to speak anywhere that I had the computer if I couldn't or didn't want to.

Autistic people have been typing for a long time, but I was told that those weren't Autistic people "like me". But oh were they like me. Typing makes communication possible when communication is impossible, even if the person I am talking to is right there. This is a thing that I was stuck on for a while, and then I had a series of seizures that made speech difficult for days & everyone had to cope.

My ibook didn't call my cats, either. But it was a portable voice when the one in my larynx wasn't doing its job.

My personal computers have gotten smaller and smaller, as have most everyone, and then, in 2008…I finally got a phone.

I didn't want a phone. I don't like phones. I do not like talking on them. People on the other end don't understand me & the feeling is mutual. But you know what was finally becoming standard? Unlimited text messages, that's what.

I don't call. I do text. A phone call that would take an hour because of speech & auditory processing issues can be handled much less stressfully over text messages. It's amazing. I text people who are sitting next to me sometimes. And I can text people who I must deal with but who would be weird about my netbook or tablet. It's amazing. I haven't had to speak to anyone on the phone for 6 months as of this writing. "I prefer to text" is an accommodation that is assumed to be a generational thing, instead of something stemming from difficulty accessing speech. It shouldn't matter, but explaining to bosses and such is not likely to go well. "But think of the children!" hides a lot of bigotry.

My cat doesn't text, unfortunately.

And now I have a tablet. Tablets solve autism, don't you know?

That isn't true. There's nothing to solve. But they *do* have a number of augmentive & alternative communication apps. I have several. Were I a child now I'd likely be denied AAC for the same reason it didn't occur to anyone that the words I typed on my mother's typewriter mattered (I had verbal speech! Assistive tech unneccesary!), but it would have helped so much in some situations. In addition to having online friends, connectivity to them nearly everywhere, and options to synchronous and asynchronous communications—I have options for when I just had a seizure and can't speak or write, and I have options for when talking is just too hard. My tablet has 2 general apps—a text to words one and one that has pictures and programmed in words—and it has a couple of situation specific apps.

It's pretty freeing, carrying a device that weighs less than a pound that has my "help" issues and also some good solid insults all programmed in. It's the little things in life.

Had you told me just before I met the internet that I would say things and people would listen, and that I would be ok even if I had seizures while alone in public I would think you were making fun of me. Had you told me just after I met the internet that in 15 years the vast majority of my communications would be typed, I'd think that was the impossible dream. And if you had told me that everyone would communicate with me via text? I would have cried because I so badly wanted it to be true, but a cat coming when called by a computer would have been the least improbable part of the scenario for me.

…and yet here we are. It's all true. Even the part about my cat.

Loud Voices
Kayla Miki Takeuchi

I was born in silence. For 15 long years I was unable to communicate even the simplest ideas. School was a complete waste of time. My parents did everything they could to find a way for me to have a voice. Finally, my doctor recommended me to a lady who works with silent people through typing. It took my mom six months to call her; in fact my doctor called her and made my mom set up the appointment.

My real birthday is April 3, 2007. I will never forget how I typed for three hours that first time. My parents were in shock to say the least. During our ride home I will never forget listening to my parents talking about what I had done. This was the true beginning of my transformed life.

I trained my mom right away so I could set new life goals. I first enrolled in a charter high school so I could get a real diploma. I received my real high school diploma and then enrolled in college.

College has been a wonderful challenge. I have really learned so much about a variety of topics. Having a voice has allowed me to participate in the world in many great ways. I have been the guest speaker several times. I participate in a group of typers called Loud Talking Fingers, and we meet monthly to discuss our lives and do social things together. I have a wonderful life because I can communicate not only simple wants and needs, but also complex feelings and thoughts that make up a complete life.

Communication is the foundation for all things in life. If I did not have a voice, I would be nothing more than a shell of a person being led around. I really want to encourage those who work with the voiceless to always presume competence to ensure that they reach their highest potential.

Keys
Aleph Altman-Mills

They took my mouth.
Split my lips into social scripts,
poured shoe polish words down my throat
I still can't stop coughing up.
My mouth is a wind up toy,
and I do not have the key.
My mouth thinks it can change
laughing at me to laughing with me
simply by laughing along.

They never took my hands.
They tried to.
My hands fell into my lap, played dead
until their glow-in-the-dark eyes disappeared.
Alone, they resurrected,
mapped my heart on paper,
played hopscotch on a computer keyboard.

My hands have pulled me out of so many swamps.
I type orange juice, and my legs re-ravel,
suddenly know where the fridge is.
I type breathe, and my lungs have permission.
I type a name, and now it is my own.

I type notes, paperweights,
so what I know doesn't blow off.
I type roads to what I know,
so I know what I am.
I type so I can speak:
tracks of letters, so the trains
on my tongue will not crash.
I type things that will not fit
through my keyhole of a mouth.

I'm not ashamed my hands know.
I am okay my hands know.

My hands know what I don't know how to say.

How Do I Explain?
Kimberly R. Dixon

How do I explain all things related to my life without a voice, and how do I let others know my thoughts and needs without words? From an early age, I knew I was smart, but I had no way to let people see my intelligence until I learned to communicate by typing when I was 6 years old.

When I was interviewed by Prime Time Live when I was 7, here is what I told the man filming me:

> *People often think that people who cannot talk are retarded. It is very hard to believe that people can be so pessimistic. I am not retarded. I am very sagacious. I like to type words that are difficult because I want people to know that I am intelligent.*

I continued to use facilitated communication to express myself at home, school, and in the community. One day I decided I wanted to write a poem. Here's my first poem in 1995 when I was 10:

Friends Role of Love
Awesome friends quite often call;

They love me even when I fall.
Being loved is good and kind;
Tears of joy are often mine.

Wishing I could tell how I feel
With a voice that is real.
I can type thoughts I have inside,
But it seems hard to really confide.

Always Jesus hears my prayers;
He is a friend who really cares.
He loves me all the time,
Even if I sin inside.

Friends dance across my life,
Answering my cries and strife.
I begin singing in my heart,
And naming all the friends I cart.

Opening vast oceans of love,
Being friends is like wearing a glove.
My friends hold me tight,
And keep me from fright.

Joy fills my life when friends are here;
I pray my friends will always be near.

People need to become friends with us who cannot speak so they can understand our struggles, as well as our joys. Lots of things go on in my mind that I would like time to share with a friend who can support me in my bold way of communicating.

Thanks to my main facilitator, who happens to be my mom, I have recently published a book of my poetry and art. Now, I want to attend college classes. Freedom to attend means I need facilitators to go with me. Without my method of communication, I cannot express what I know or even ask questions.

When I was in public school, it was often a battle to have a facilitator help me communicate in class. My mom and I had many meetings with school personnel about this issue. Here is a poem I wrote back then that expressed my frustration.

Fight for Freedom

Trampling fear into the ground
Americans seize the moment
And fight for freedom.
In my own life
I must overcome my fears
And fight for my right to communicate.

Quite a lot of my friends type to communicate. We all must unite and fight for our right to communicate the way we wish. In numbers, we will be able to show the world that we are not garbage, but people with hopes and dreams.They took my mouth.

❖ ❖ ❖

Invisible Man Revisited
Lateef McLeod

I am the transparent mirage in your mind's eye.
The image you want to hold,
but with time
will simply forget.

You think you see me.
Can visualize and grasp
who I am.
In a wheelchair, yes.
Use an A.A.C. device to speak, yes.
Has cerebral palsy, yes.
Was educated at U C Berkeley and Mills, yes.
Still you will not see me.

Because that is just the mask
that the real me hides behind

to give you that false security,
that my life is ok.
Must be ok!
I am a productive, working, taxpayer.
It must be ok.

But if I take off the mask
to reveal my true facial features.
Let you see how my family and friends
take me for granted
and barely stay in contact with me.

I am always the odd man out.
The one left out of informal gatherings.
Of friends chatting about old times
over good food.
Or even formal gatherings,
"You are going to this party right?
Everyone is going."
I am like "What party?"
I must have missed that on my Facebook scroll.

When close friends marry,
I am invited
of course there is no room in the bridal party.
I'm always one place removed from
the close circle of intimate community,
always
an orphan hugging myself in the wind.

When will I be accepted into relationships
where I am called when you need someone
to talk,
laugh,
or cry to?
What trial must I triumph
so that the scales fall from your eyes.
Because if I am invisible for too long
I might totally disappear for good.

❖ ❖ ❖

Inside of Me
Leonard Schwartz

Inside of me the signals never functioned in the way that I demanded. It was seen as similar to a traffic light that was not working as expected. When someone intervenes at an intersection more is understood and the level of smoothness increases. This is how I think about life before and after I was heard through spelling on a letter board. I am understood and my level of smoothness has increased.

❖ ❖ ❖

Autobiography
Lily

[**Editorial note:** *The text in italics was written by Lily's mother. The rest by Lily.*]

Autobiography: Lily
My name is Lily. I am six years old. Some people like me type because of our culture of brain.
I enjoy learning. My center is caring. I am quite determined.
Caring about each other will let everyone be all they are able to be.

(What does typing mean to you?)

Typing is my expression.
It lets me share my thoughts.
I feel freedom.
It reveals my potential.
Typing is excellent for my culture of brain.
Not everyone is very understanding in letting children be who we are intended to be.

(Poem)

"Every touch"

Every touch finds excellent release of pleasing feelings.
Each one impossibly endeavoring to create understanding in me.
Each teaches quite beautiful intense new feelings of safety and peace.

I can sense unseen often attractive things pleasing to my hand.
Touch is my expression to tell and feel the beauty of my world.
Touch lets me find my inner excellent control.

My touch is quite extraordinary.

(Poem written on contemplating ancient bristlecone pine trees)

"Living Tree"

Old when Mesopotamia was young.
Leaning against rocks fighting no one.
Living very quiet.
Freedom.

(Realistic fiction - as Lily explained: "I endeavored to tell a fun story")

"Ian goes fishing"

Ian went to the river to go fishing. He played his guitar. A fish splashed in
the river.
Ian endeavored to catch the fish. The fish was most determined to flee and
it swam quickly into a underwater cave.
Ian felt disappointed and he went on a walk to figure and think about how
to tell his entire family how the fish jumped and escaped.

Lucy's Song 2007
Lucy Blackman

The water flows my brain.
It flows through and flows past.
It flows in and whirlpools round.

Water carries pebbles
And the grinding of stones
Is the nucleus of thought.
Destruction builds sediment and
 the sentient sediment
.... is emotion in the raw.
Somehow ...
We have to channel sludge
Back to the rainbow sands.
That is the role of words.
Words are worship – praise – shopping lists – possibly lies
And always the wonder of us humans as hairless mammals,
Somehow greater than angels in our despair and humour.
That is my song.   (Written February 2007)

****

Lucy's Song is the end of long path, though I cannot see the stile over which I shall go on to the next stage of my journey.

I was 14 years old, and had never written or spoken coherently when I first used a Canon Communicator. Six weeks later I wrote my third poem, drawing from my mind blotches of colour and wisps of sound to create words. I called it *A Happy Poem.*

****

Make me another world,
A world where I can sing,
Another world where the towns
Are bright in the sun.
Does the sun shine
On rainy days in another world?
Does the road go on into another world
Where I can talk and sing?   (March 1987)

****

In 1992, the year in which I turned 20 and the year in which the narrative of my autobiography ends, my hearing responded to an alternative treatment. I suddenly lost all interior music in the sense of lyrical autistic sound. I talk about this in the last chapters of *Lucy's Story.*

"For past failings, the sound ran like a chaotic sludge.
That is the way I feel about language.
Chaotic sludge transforms to clarity in intent, but not the sight.

(March 1992)

That was the last attempt I ever made to write a poem. My inside language had changed completely. Previously my mind and my voice had warbled and cooed in unison, and my typed language and my visual words were positively reinforced by that magical process. That is, both my noises and my occasional spoken words had been completely separate from thought. Occasionally from this time on, the words I uttered meant something to the listener, though really they were only labels or requests. In a path to rather more typical language processing, I lost the most precious gift of the poetry of thought, of a dancing and swooping mind and body.

Of course I still had most wonderful control of words and I drew great pleasure from fluent prose writing, but had more thought-work in putting the characters in my brain through my finger and onto a screen. In my mind I had words, but I had not retained the gift of autistic enjoyment to the extent I had before." (*Lucy's Story*, p. 279)

Most of the next fifteen years were really a continual path to typing with minimal physical contact, not because I personally thought it important but because it was essential if I was to establish my own achievement in the eyes of others.

I had to concentrate on the discipline of writing for university courses. That is completely different from high school work, and in many ways completely removed from practical communication. The fact is that I can express complex thoughts but not practical information. So in writing about a scene which I have created for a story, I revisit the draft several times and laboriously build it up in increments. An ordinary thinker would imagine a narrative and then fill in the gaps. So really I am building in patterns. Other writers seem to write to communicate something they want another person to visualize.

Then in Brisbane, nearly twenty years after gaining language, I came to meet with people who also finger their language. I joined The Brotherhood of the Wordless. We see each other once a month and write from the imagination rather than pass on facts as conventional people seem to think is important. It is in this big airy room in a Community Centre near a rail line that I have rediscovered music in sight and words in finger feeling.

That is so abstract! Can I suggest that people with autistic spectrum differences, even those using coherent speech, often appear abstract when they are describing what to them is concrete world-experiencing. If this is something which does happen, it solves complex questions about supported typing in people like me.

This suggests to me that possession of the changing challenge of ASD is indeed the springboard to creativity? I think that for me the most interesting reality in my life is the relationship between facilitation and autism. My intelligence is expressed in different thought processes from most people.

You see, technically I don't have a physical disability. I can tie my shoes, make a sandwich, wash up and hang laundry. They are not a series of deliberate actions but a compulsive and impulsive ritual of something I have mastered. So it is not surprising that I do have problems with complex skills like cooking a meal or even making the right movements in response to a timer or a visual schedule.

To be a person without speech and with autistic behaviours is the most interesting scenario! The whole world is reduced to Mr. Bean as the rest of God's creation navigates my universe.

Instead of my Bean image, one could say that people without ASD or other movement differences strand themselves on the beaches of my behaviour. What a very funny image that is. Behaviour is an abstract and the whale image is a metaphor. Really, totally enchanted though I am with this, I must stop wallowing to make it clear that I am coming to the point.

Movement is the characteristic with which we associate intellectual disability. With that come the anxieties of those responsible for our wellbeing. They see us as vulnerable on the one hand, or as being incapable of measuring the subtle needs of the school or adult environment.

For what is speech? It has nothing to do with intelligence in its most basic form. It is simply a highly specialized motor movement only available to this one species. Can other animals see it as significant? Have deer any idea that antlers are not attractive to other species? And how does a dog socialize if it has no sense of smell? It is a disability which would not be obvious to a human, but the downstream effects in behavior would seem like some kind of psychological disorder!

Changing mental and physical impulses in sync is terribly complicated. In fact some people find it impossible, and given the importance that changing contemporary culture places on presentation within a social context, one could say that people with autism are possibly more distinguishable today than at any other time in history—or pre-history! (By autism I mean also the larger group of people in the diagnostic category of PDD.)

It is so funny—that is to say it is "funny" both in the sense of "funny-peculiar" and "funny-haha" as my granny used to say—that the non-autistic have social problems in uncovering the sense of autistic communication!

For many people facilitation—that is assistance in concentration and making sense of body movement—is the nearest they come to interaction. And it is also funny (in both senses) that the principal objection—but have to say not the only objection—to hands-on support is the possibility of influence, and the likely feeling of close emotional connection, both of which are typically deficits in autistic relationships!

Can you imagine the excitement if a non-speaking man with severe behaviour problems reacted to affectionate touch or subtle communication prompts? That is the response which facilitators report, and yet is disparaged as having a deleterious effect by the people who demand communication without facilitation.

The function of language is only in part communication. The function of my language is to change my chaotic thoughts into an internal coherent universe where I can be at peace. To do that, I have to type regularly in a structured setting and feel safe in my understanding. That is Nirvana for me.

For me conversation is chaos in time and sound. To steal from the annals of philosophy, I think in words, therefore thought is mine.

****

❖ ❖ ❖

I Am A 43-Year-Old Autistic Adult
Mandy Klein

I am a 43-year-old autistic adult diagnosed in my early thirties.

I have always struggled to communicate, especially by speaking. Some people would say I am shy. I'm not so sure. I know I am always fearful of doing and saying the wrong thing.

I do know that I'm autistic and I also know that there are many times when I can't speak no matter how much I want to.

When Facebook and email came out, they opened up a completely new world to me. I could suddenly 'talk' to people. There are times where it can still take me a few days to reply to messages because I have to process what the other person wrote or it is a hard subject for me to figure out.

I have made friends on Facebook whom I would never have made in real life. I have very few real life friends. The more I message my Facebook friends or comment on their posts, the more I feel comfortable. I would love to meet many of these people, especially the one who are autistic like me but I probably wouldn't be able to say much to them in person! Not verbally anyway. They would be understanding and maybe I would have the courage to use text-to-speech with them.

I really struggle with phone calls. I always check if the person or company I need to contact has an email address first. I am more likely to get my point across properly that way. Many companies don't even answer their emails though. If I have to talk on the phone or in person, I lose my words and stumble around, even if I have a script written.

Talking to people verbally face to face and on the phone requires quick processing speed. There are many times and situations where I just don't have what is required. I end up agreeing to things I don't want to. If I know the person well, this isn't as likely to happen, especially if they are aware of the problem and are checking to make sure it is something I really want.

My daughter (and husband) is also autistic, so I attend parent support groups. There are usually quite a few parents in the one group and I usually cannot talk. My verbal ability goes down according to my anxiety levels i.e. more people, less talking and/or new people less talking. It can be very frustrating, especially if they are saying something about their autistic child that needs to be corrected, so they understand the autistic point of view. My autism consultant currently runs the group and if I am up to it, I can pass her a note with what I want to say and she will say it for me.

It is difficult for me when I disagree with people because I cannot verbally debate them on topics, no matter how badly I want to or how well I know the subject. I can on the internet when I type though!

It is hard when you have been brought up to have to answer verbally. It was very embarrassing in school being forced to answer questions verbally. I always made a mess of it.

I do have text-to-speech apps but have not had the courage to use them yet. It is a struggle when people know you can speak. What they don't understand is that it is hard to speak in a way that they will understand, to process what they are saying, deal with sensory issues, and multiple other things at the same time. For most allistic people, that is just something that is automatic. There is such stigma around autism. People may see a speaking autistic who has to use AAC and think 'what a faker' or 'she can talk, don't let her use that, she doesn't need it'. This has never happened to me personally (because I haven't tried it much yet), but I do know it happens. I want to feel free and not scared to openly use something that will help me.

I didn't even text when I first got my iPhone. My autism consultant got me started on that. She uses it a lot and when I first met her, I wasn't sure if I could talk to her because there ended up being a sudden transition from another consultant whom I had had for years. It was my new consultant's idea that if I couldn't speak in our meetings, I could text or we could use Facebook message.

Another way that typing has helped me is with my blog. I am able to say things, especially about my feelings that I cannot get out through my mouth. Sometimes, it can take weeks to get it out even by typing, but it does come. If I was trying to speak, it would never come out. I have noticed that when I am upset about something, if I blog about it as soon as possible, I am able to get my real feelings and frustrations out. This is a new and helpful thing. It is helping me to become a better advocate for others and myself. The words are starting to come out through the keyboard, but it has to be done as soon as possible, otherwise the words disappear. I also have to be careful because certain people may read what I write and get worried (this has happened even though there is no reason to be). I am tempted to start another blog but keep it anonymous so that I can say whatever I need to say. It would be interesting to see what would happen if I had that freedom. Something I have definitely never had with the spoken word.

I am more misunderstood when I speak with my mouth. I have trouble regulating my tone of voice and can't understand other people's tone of voice then you add in the jumbled up words and things can get messy. You don't have that problem in writing.

There are those of us who struggle with understanding when something is sarcasm, therefore the sarcastic phrase should have the word sarcasm in brackets beside it, if someone is being sarcastic. It makes things more clear. If what has been written is a joke, then write joking in brackets. I think I am getting a little clearer with my writing that way.

I am a member of an autistic adult advisory committee for a local autism organization and they are very understanding of my communication issues. It is a small group, but I can only do some verbal speaking when there are very few of us (three or four maybe), otherwise I send notes ahead of time to the facilitators and sit beside one of them so that I can write notes as needed.

To many people, I may not seem like the type of person who needs AAC. I do. It has become an important part of my life and if you say, you accept me as I am; autism and all, then you must accept that part of me also.

I am trying to be kinder and allow myself to do what I need to make my life more comfortable and to be able to access and participate in all that society has to offer. Typing has been a big part of making this possible for me. It is opening up the world to me. I am also meeting many people like me this way.

❖ ❖ ❖

Lights Inside Getting Out and Shining
Mark Utter

I am delighted to be asked to submit something to this important publication.

I have been someone profoundly affected by not being able to communicate. I always wanted to be part of what was going on around me but got no avenues of access aside from what people made up for me. People say I resemble Charlie Chaplin and in the focusing on my rote gestures this is an apt association.

I am happy to declare that I followed Chaplin's big footsteps in another way and that was to use my developing skills in Supported Typing to write, direct and star in my own movie. It shows me and the ways I don't fit in to daily life unless I am able to access my mind and share its content by painstakingly typing my thoughts. It's called "I am in here; a view of my daily life with intelligent suggestions for improvement from my intelligent mind.

After the process of producing that film I experienced a greater sense of participation in my life. I also had an invitation to Syracuse University's Center for Inclusion and Communication's Summer institute. It is here that I found members of my own culture. I am delighted to feel solidarity with this group and have moments of feeling like a leader and a mentor.

Please check out my work at www.utterenergy.org and you can learn more about my movie and sign up for my blog.

The best thing about this is that all of us in this book have had miracles happen in our lives.

Because of this we believe in them.

Mark Utter is a native Vermonter who has a form of autism and types to communicate. When Mark was first introduced to a form of alternative communication called "supported typing" he found it tedious and did not see much use for it. One day Emily asked him if he would consider using supported typing with her to write some lines for the play, "I'll Fly Away." Through this experience Mark found that he could use Supported Typing to share his story and asked Emily to support these efforts. What was intended to be a play blossomed into the film "I am in here; a view of my daily life with good suggestions for improvement from my intelligent mind." Mark has shown his movie 30 times and conducted inspirational conversations with audience members after each screening. Mark has also facilitated several workshops, has started a blog and has a new writing project in the works.

I'm On A New Awakening
Mekhi T. Shockley

I'm on a new awakening. I want everyone to know I'm not stupid. I read write and listen to music. I like Country, R&B and Christian music. I'm a good brother son and friend. I'm blessed for my gifts. I'm a child of God, I'm a passage for his word. I'm a living rein to tell the Gospel in the end days.

Story
Michael Lee

Story:
I WAS MISERABLE BEFORE I COULD SPELL. MOM ASKED FOR A GOOD RPM TEACHER TO HELP ME.

"I MIGHT MAKE THE HEADLINES," I THOUGHT.

MY MOM SAID THE SAME THING.

"HELP MY BOY," MY MOM SAID TO THE TEACHER IN SCHOOL.

"HE CAN'T LEARN," THEY SAID.

"HE IS NOT A STUPID BOY," SAID MOM "REALLY HE IS SMART."

"NO, MY STUDENTS ARE STUPID." THEY ALL SAID.

"HOW DARE YOU SAY THAT!' SAID MOM, "RIGHT NOW ASK HIM A QUESTION BEFORE A LITTLE FIGHT."

"I AM NOT GOING TO ANSWER," I THOUGHT, "HOW CAN I? THEY DON'T BELIEVE. I AM NOT GOING TO HAVE FUN HERE."

BUT THEN I HAD A NEW TEACHER COME TO MY RESCUE. SHE TAUGHT ME TO SPELL MY THOUGHTS. I DID NOT HAVE TO PROVE MY THOUGHTS WERE SMART.

"CAN THIS BELIEVING TEACHER BE MY TEACHER ALWAYS?" I THOUGHT. "CAN SHE HAVE HER PRICES LOWER?"

"HAVE A NICE DAY," I THOUGHT AS I LEFT THE SCHOOL SYSTEM.

NO ONE HAD MORE TO THINK THAN ME. I AM SPECIAL IN THE HEAD IN A GOOD WAY. I CAN THINK THINGS IN THE MOST CREATIVE WAY. I AM SMART IN MATH AND SCIENCE. HAVING A WAY TO SPELL HAS CHANGED MY LIFE.

In my head no one can be
My head is me
I can't talk well
Home can tell
My life is talking free
I am not lazy
Don't drive me crazy
No one types like me
No I am not mad
I am not bad
Typing makes me free

❖ ❖ ❖

Face My Morning Face
Michael Scott Monje, Jr.

(An Essay About Grammar Accessibility)

I am sick of posting performances for normally normative audiences, so for once I will give you this—my morning face.

> The broken syntax
> of my poetry
> is not craft
> so much as nature's way
> of communicating
> straight from my brain
> to the airwaves

It's the sentences in standard written English that have to be crafted to your expectations.

This is why, when I teach your children, I won't mark their errors.

This isn't a joke, it's rhetorical performance.

If I were to hold a grammar bee, it would have to be Grammar B.

Do you see? Your standard expectations are accessibility issues. I conform to teach you. That is not who I am though, so when you state that my brain is high-functioning, you're actually attempting to reward me for leaving it chained.

I spoke in my voice once, and everyone thought I was insane.

My lyrical echoes in assonance did not perform the transitions they looked for in relationship language, so they missed the connections in my organizational language.

This led to my great awakening. That point at which "conform or die" became "conform" and I saw that by showing off my ability to mimic norms, I could access the methods by with they are aborted.

My highest functioning trait is my ability to infiltrate.

This is not a post about neurodiversity, it's a post about rewriting the expectations of the university.

[Did we stop recognizing that *Finnegan's Wake* is not to be read as fiction because it was an entry into the New Critics' analytical debate?]

The simple semiotics of Standard Written English are too restrictive.

All of you know this, and wish I could pour these thoughts into peer review. I love you, for your encouragement, but can not get into it.

I don't receive enough Grammar A hours in my day to do it.

The best I can do is to show you through the poetry, and maybe put parables into published stories.

This is my morning face. The unmedicated, untutored output of my real brain.

This is my high function.

In an hour it will slip through fingers and run down the shower drain as my maintenance chemicals squash the anxiety that allows for this kind of lyrical/logical fusion. The dissolution of my true nature is necessary to imitate the behavior of my colleagues long enough to get paid.

It's not that I can't do it. You've seen the other essays.

It's just the things I do to myself to accomplish those ends are often costly. If you didn't have such expectations about what was cognitively accessible to your people, we could have a deeper conversation.

As it is, I am happy to translate myself for you. The cost of my doing this is that occasionally I will make you glimpse the original dialect, complete with specific example deficits and accomplished, polished echolalaic statements.

Sometimes you just have to have redundant language. To lose it might focus your argument, but it will prevent the movement in your cadence from taking flight.

Try it sometime. You just might like baroque dialogue and token phrasings given over more to rhetorical rhythm than supporting claims.

I have a confession.

Your semiotic systems are not complex enough to capture my rhythms. I guarantee this. I've been studying them.

When you encounter nonsense babbling from children you think you're not reaching, remember me.

Chances are they are spouting multi-dimensional symbols with definitions you're not reaching.

I learned your language.

How many half-measures can you still call teaching?

Sorry. Not meaning to insult anyone there, but dad was an asshole and we are all the products of what we've been taught.

Final thought:
I am only disabled because the cognitive basis of my language is not accessible to those who don't already speak it. I would be happy to teach it, but it is taught as the basis for discrimination and a presumption of incompetence, so no one wants to speak it. Your attempts to teach are well-meaning, but ultimately fail because you're demanding I learn how you speak without learning the vocabulary to translate for me.

Fín

Painting On My Performance Face

Michael Scott Monje, Jr.

(An Essay About Gender and Sensory Language Processing)

This is a reflection on my earlier morning face essay, written in a space where I had been forced to perform socially in a persona and still had solitude after to meditate on the processes by which I communicate.

This is also the ninth installment in my Thoughts On Writing series, and it is a parable, a narrative, and a direct confessional in response to the promptings of another round of meditation on William Burroughs. Receive it as you will, but never seek to see if it is literal. The beings speaking here are giving you their only meaning.

*"**Naked Lunch** demands Silence from The Reader."*

* * *

I'm painting on my performance face,
that rhetorical visual that is super-lingual,
a schooled posture of tongues and jaws,
eyebrow arches and permissively
self-indulgent
facial tics
all covered over with a caking makeup mask
meant to reveal that which my
previous self-images
forced to remain hidden.

I breathe in
mineral fumes
suspended in talcum
like mudpies
in the back
of my throat
or sand in my lungs
and it makes my
central nervous system
hum.

It's him awakening to place his face behind my mask
like the task master,
puppet masturbating
high femme
narcissistic
scum
I always wanted to see
him be.

Don't worry about me,
my language is meant to be embarrassing.
He won't let it get to him,
and other than that
I leave it to you to conclude
your own intuitions about our
relationship.

So I paint him into being,
my high femme alter ego,
a boy who always wished
he'd been born in the time of The Cure
and not the time of Phish.

It's ironic, isn't it?
That I actually wouldn't want to
paint this face
if not for the fact that my face
isn't even in the same place
I think it should be,
much less does it reflect
my self-image
hormonally.

I'd rather,
in all honesty,
be butchy,
but the personality I crafted for me
to interact with the outside world
is dysphoric,
and his annoying
gender nonconformity

won't leave me to be me.

That was why I finally summoned the energy
to speak Me
into being.

Not that I had not tried to communicate…
If anything,
this stylistic fetish of his is because of things I did,
like when we were kids
and I wanted him to see
he was meant to be listening to me,
so I would make him shriek
and shy away from dirty play
by playing up his perceptions from his senses
until he couldn't process what was coming from which direction.
It wasn't personal.
I did it because I couldn't say
my say any other way.
In fact, I'm nonverbal to this day.
I type to communicate.

I tried to speak,
but the only way my body
will get to talking
is if I'm singing
or I'm acting,
and acting like a girl is hard on me
because my voice is
capable
of a range
that is quite comfortable,
even with a dysphoric hormonal balance,
and it wouldn't improve with help
in any way but strength.

Unfortunately for me,
thirty years of testosterone
and cigarettes
have honed my tone,
and now I am trapped
with his nasal-but-low vocals

if I ever want to speak smoothly
without singing.
And singing is out for me,
with my throat whistling
like a weak reed,
or a six year old's ghost
in old-school-pastiche-nouveau
hipster horror movies,
right before the inappropriately
incestuous scene
that they all seem
to be moving
toward including
ever since Spike Lee
remade that *Oldboy*
movie.

So I'm trapped in my body,
embodying
a speaking personality
who isn't me,
but who
for some reason
lines up with my anatomy,
and I can remember
making him as I was closeting,
but I can't rightly say that he is me...
...and at night, in the dark, when we're talking
he whispers
that his existence is fictive
but still relevant
and I can't deny
his reasoning is strong...

...and he keeps telling me
that killing him
would be wrong.

So I sequester myself inside text messages,
seizing his career's reigns,
making my meaning
through his body

even if I can't kick him out of his place
in the brain
that allows us to speak.

My sentient hologram,
my singularity AI,
resonating in the firmware
of my chemical mainframe
and flipping the bird
at Ray Kurzweil.
He's not a multiple or divergent
personality.
We both agree:
I made him.
He is me.
I'm just not him,
and he's not listening.
So sometimes I can only be myself
when I keep him at home,
where he can't speak.
Online teaching can be good for this,
see?

But the truth is,
there is a truce
we can live with.
If I leave him his rhetorical station,
he thinks his dysphoria will be cured once I start my hormonal intervention.

That means we're pulling together now,
a marriage of an autistic trans humanist
and her neurotypical golem children,
animated rhetorical visions of character caricatures
that ran themselves unscripted
and then went to school for improv lessons
to learn to blend in to social relationships.

I'm only speaking when I'm seeing a screen,
and I can find my voice in my fingertips
when I have a rhythm,
like how I wrote this missive
to Gangstagrass

and then it switched to Creedence,
and my lines got longer
and I played a little more with dissonance.

I can't do this if he's talking,
and he can't speak if I'm engaged.
Any attempt to break this agreement leaves us enraged
and though I'm mature enough now not to tear around the place,
I come from a family of high anxiety
and cardiovascular problems,
and I don't want to place myself on pace
to need a pacemaker
before I have gray hair
or lines on my face
that my makeup
can't smooth
and replace.

So I need to keep my peace to keep my pace
in a professional race
that's only gotten tighter and tougher
since I first failed to place
myself in its space,
during a previous fistfight with dysphoria
when I did not manage
to break his grip on our hands
and free my voice.

I've had to forcibly negotiate
with my own face
to figure out my pace
and my place,
which interventions I can tolerate,
and how my health might deteriorate,
and which interventions I could tolerate replacing
if I don't make my way into a more lucrative situation
before the day comes that I lose more range of motion...

...I'm not complaining, I'm just saying...

...I'm already so stiff with the strains and breaks
of this historically abusive relationship...

But I can do this.
And we're finally getting through this,
now that his cognitive processes
have academically precise scripts
that allow him to describe embodied knowledge
I have so much confidence
that I'm going to let him edit this,
and I bet he still decides to send it.

But before I flee to let him read so he can speak,
I want to describe how this takes place.
We're both here and seeing,
but I can't process my language if he's speaking,
and he can't converse with people
or think about what to say next
If I'm in the middle of composing a text.
So, we have to read everything twice.
Once in silence, without intrusion.
Once in group social situations,
to situate our perceptions.

The problem is I can't make him realize it
until we get alone so he'll be quiet
and then I find my voice and I weak reed it,
because I can sing even if I can't speak it,
and I can compose strings of rhythmic syllables
by holding on to cracks between consonants
until I can drop to the next vowel in our progression.

When I do this,
I can only hope I make sense,
so I tend to ramble a bit
because I don't know the word I want,
I only know the sensation of making it.

This is where my flow went when I got back into academics, when I had to get
competitive.
When I got afraid to walk away from my dad's family,
and my partner got sick and I got too cowardly to live openly.

But that's not fair to me.

I was doing what was needed
to keep hold of her
like I knew she would
keep hold of me,
and I was making,
like,
fourteen thousand
dollars a year
and living in hospitals on weekends.
Who could afford to be authentic under those conditions?

So I swallowed my pride and performed my body's normative social projections
and even believed they were for the best for a time,
until I'd almost talked myself into a position of relative influence,
and my realization of the proximity of the resources
that would give me the power to change my performance
made me try to assert myself prematurely,
and I'd go nonverbal in job interviews because I had to prove I could do it
because I know I'm a lot smarter than him.

And he would get mad when I'd do this.
And I would hit him or break things.
It took a diagnosis and a process of years for us to reach this point,
and he's happy to let me call the shots,
as long as I let him express himself professionally.

He's the teacher.

I'm the... me.

He's going to get us back into an academic position,
and I'm the household tenure review committee.

Now watch out.
I'm coming.

* * *

Know this, its space, and the way that once you close the document it will blink out of existence.

Origin stories are rhetorical performances.

I swear it.

❖ ❖ ❖

My Many Communication Systems

Anonymous

The person who wrote this can talk and can write. The person who wrote this does not speak all the time. The person who wrote this wishes to remain anonymous because of very real concerns about employment discrimination. This person has experienced discrimination by people who do not understand communication differences. This person sometimes talks in a very non-typical way. This person is very careful to try to talk in "the regular way" in order to not attract any negative attention at work or in places where WORD might get back to the workplace.

I have struggled for months with this essay. Finally, I decided to do it anonymously, although some people may figure out it's *me*. My reason for writing anonymously is that my employment requires me to be a professional communicator, including speaking to groups and doing interpersonal relations communications. I am able to pull it off well enough to work, but I create my own behind-the-scenes accommodations rather than requesting them directly. A few times I made requests and was denied so not thinking I will put in my name as it might be problematic for me. Hopefully, I can make a difference even when not willing to say who I am. The ideal thing would be to both state who I am *and* write what I am going to say here, so that people can see the entire picture of who I am and the different ways I communicate. Unfortunately, I am semi-closeted when it comes to the more unusual ways I communicate, because I fear that I will have difficulty with employment. I do want to show readers here that I have a varying ability to speak, to speak and use "standard syntax," to speak and find the "correct" words, to speak at all. Being anonymous lets me be more revealing about my language use even as I do not reveal who I am. I hope it will help other Autistics think about their own communication in ways that are useful.

Not one thing in this article should be interpreted to mean that I cannot ever communicate my exact thoughts to people, in both talking and writing. It sometimes takes longer, or has to happen at another time, or requires the use of alternatives to talking. I want to preempt anyone thinking that they can dismiss what I say or write, or that they need to jump in and "interpret" me to others.

Spoken language is almost completely reliable when I have a public speaking engagement or am at an employment venue that requires me to talk. Speaking in public or at a meeting has a time limit, so I can usually succeed, because it happens over a period of an hour or maybe several hours (and in a couple of cases, some two- or three-day conferences with very few breaks, but I was not the only one talking). I have divided my communications into several types. I use writing, some ASL, voice recorder apps, text-to-speech apps, and nonstandard speech and syntax.

Writing: Sometimes I can write to people instead of talking. If I am at a computer or have paper and pen/pencil, or one of several text-to-speech apps on my iPhone, writing is usually easy. Writing while out in public, or even with people I am having private conversations with, quickly becomes very tedious. Typing, even fast typing, is much slower than speech. My handwriting is about 20 words per minute, so if I am writing something out, my communication partner is going to have a much longer wait than if I were speaking at the speed of a recorded audio book, or about 160 wpm. Typing is about 50-80 wpm. My own typing is about 68 wpm when I am typing fast. This means that speech is typically twice as fast as writing, for me. Communication partners who are not able or, sometimes, not willing to use asynchronous forms of language-based communication such as instant messaging might have to wait longer for me to write something down. With instant messaging, chat, and even email, a communication can take less time because we can overlap each other and figure it out as we go along. Sure, there are times when the communicators have to back up and figure out who is answering what, but that happens with spoken conversations, too. Don't assume that because someone is communicating at 20-70 wpm instead of 150 that they are "dumb." It just means it is taking longer. I am talking about "real time" conversations here. Given the chance to write a one-page communication, and have the other person read it and write their own page back, amazing communications can happen. One benefit of having the other communication partner put things in text is that I can think about what they said, a huge help when it comes to auditory processing disabilities, sequencing, short-term memory, and other areas in which Autistic people like me often have trouble.

American Sign Language: I am learning American Sign Language. It is a new language for me. I am learning it primarily as another way to communicate with my child. My child is taking an ASL class with me. One of the first things he asked me, in fingerspelling, looked like "R-B-A-L," and I could not get what he meant. I was sounding each letter out loud trying to figure it out. "N?" "R-B-L?" Um, "N--V--R-B-L?" Finally he said "Mom, nonverbal?" I said "I guess not, since I was saying the letters out loud!" We had a good laugh about that. My child sometimes asks "Nonverbal?" when he is trying to see if I can talk or not. ASL is becoming one more non-speaking form of communication that we can use.

Voice recorder: Another AAC tool I have is a voice recorder app. Since I *can* talk at times, I make pre-recorded "answers" to questions people might ask. These have the advantage of being recorded in my own voice. Using the recorder in this way is similar to text-to-speech generation in that the other person will be able to hear what I say, but it's me saying it, even though it was recorded in the past. One interesting development came from recording some phrases I thought I might need to use when nonspeaking or having difficulty with speech production. I then found some of the phrases easier to use when I was speaking. I started recording phrases like "Excuse me. I am not finished talking," and playing them over and over, hearing them in my own voice. As a person who often cannot calculate exactly *when* to interrupt (in the case of someone not taking turns very well, or actively trying to keep me out of a conversation, or in meetings with many participants) having these phrases in my own voice and hearing them myself has made it easier to use them when I need to. Some other examples are: "That is *not* what I meant." "That is *exactly* what I meant " (because sometimes people think I am implying something rather than stating it, and they come up with some amazing things that I "really meant" instead of what I just said!). Shortly after I started recording phrases and sentences on the voice recorder, I had to be on the phone to resolve a business matter. The person on the phone was talking over me and not letting me finish. I said "Excuse me, I am not finished talking," which was one of my recorded phrases I had been listening to. I was a bit amazed at myself, because I often just wait until the other person stops, if they ever do! I have not been able to use text-to-speech apps as much as I would like. Unless I set the volume exactly right, it is hard to hear in a public space, and people have a hard time realizing they need to listen to the speaker (the speaker accessory plugged into the iPhone) and not look at me expectantly, thinking I am going to talk.

Please do not think an app is going to teach your child or your family member, or maybe you, to speak out of their mouth. It might. It might not. I am talking about *my own* communication differences. I could only be talking about *your* communication differences, and perhaps those of your family member (but be careful when assuming "I am like your child") if you find something in my words here that makes sense to you, that parallels your own experience, or that you can put into practice or modify according to your own needs.

Speaking. What do I do? I can mostly use speech at work. I am so happy that I do not have to talk nonstop at work! When I can't speak, I am often able divert communications to email.

If there came a point where communication systems completely broke down, I feel it would be my responsibility to let people know that I needed to communicate another way. "Typical" people have no idea that someone might not be able to talk, so I need to tell them. You might think it would be the other way around, or that they should ask, but in my experience, that rarely happens, so it's up to me to communicate about the situation. For some Autistics, this step is not possible. Communication partners who know that an Autistic person might not be able to speak need to check to make sure the person has a way of communicating. This does *not* mean taking over or presuming to know what the person wants or means, rushing the person, demanding that they only use speech. It requires a lot of thoughtfulness and can result in some miscommunications. If both communication partners are committed to making communications work their best, communication can proceed. When one communication partner refuses to adopt any alternatives to speech, communication can be thwarted, sometimes for a long time. I have had this happen to me on a number of occasions.

Nonstandard speech and syntax: Sometimes my spoken communications come out of my mouth in an unusual (to most people) order. Some times this happens because I am talking faster than I can find words. It also happens when I am tired or overloaded, or even when I can't be bothered with having to think of "regular sentences."

It is *not* that I don't understand how language works, including metaphors, similes, and most figures of speech. I would not be writing this sentence if I did not. It is the *speaking* part of language that is often difficult or impossible, and it is the using of language in fast-paced conversations that is troublesome, not the use of language in a thoughtful, written, form that can be edited to my liking before letting anyone see it. When I attend conferences or meetings with many people, and which proceed at a fairly fast pace, you will see me scribbling furiously (and listening as best I can at the same time) in order to have a script for my comments. I then will find an appropriate place in the conversation and add my thoughts. At times I have said "My comments are addressing something that was said about five minutes ago, but I needed to write it down." Some conferences have been a bit less accommodating, and are more of a struggle. Personal and private communications vary a lot.

I looked up the definition of syntax and found this: "The arrangement of words and phrases to create well-formed sentences in a language." If that is the definition of syntax, I would say that my syntax, rather than conforming to "well-formed" English, is in its own category, partially shared by some other Autistics whose writings I have encountered, and who may have some influence on my own use of words and ordering of them.

My child says "Mom, it's like you have invented a new language. It's not that hard to understand. Anyone could do it if they tried." I am quite fortunate to have a child who is not disturbed by my idiosyncratic word use. One thing I do is taking "around" something, usually a noun I have not thought of yet, and finally come to that noun after describing it in detail, often using only one- or two-syllable descriptors. I seem to add extra prepositions, too.

Here are some examples:

"All the dishes. Make them go into a washed condition."

"I want you to do your this. It has to happen before the snowing." (It was something, obviously, that I wanted him to do before it snowed. He could understand me because I probably either pointed at the "this" or he just knew what it was because we had discussed it either in speech or writing including me typing, or us using IM, or emailing).

Regarding a loud noise: "I want it to go off! No making of it!"

Cooking directions—"Put all those pieces of bacon in there. They will smallen up and fit."

"Putting of the phone on the thing so it can cook overnight and be ready in the morning." (My child responded, "You mean the charger?!")

"I'm not talking about this anymore because it takes away from my brain." "Nonverbal because probably processing in brain is on glasses and vision and not to talking of words" (—an explanation to someone about why I was having trouble with words when I was adjusting to a new pair of glasses.)

"What is that singing sound?" (—upon hearing the phone ring.)

"Let me check my phone—I need to see what color he called me with." (This means—Let me check my phone to see what number he called from. Synesthesia, anyone?!)

"You want waffles? Let me make to you for."

"To making of dog food?"

"I told of you to doing that!"

"To dog not pestering me!" ("Dog, stop bothering me!" [begging for food].)

"To nudging of me with your nose. Making it stop!" (I guess the dog really does want something!)

"Making of the thing that goes into the trash of the laundry." ("Put that in the laundry basket.")

"Where is that thing that rings and you answer it?!" ("Where is the phone?")

"Hand me the thing that is a long thing with a handle that is long because it flips over the hamburger."

"I want to go to the place that has the food that has the crackers that is called a store."

"Needing to making go away. That big rectangle is taking up a lot of space that we don't use. That we don't play with. And also making into livingroomness and deskness.... So..... to..... that...." [trails off...] Making everything to be an office in there." (A discussion of where to move some furniture.)

"Goodbye out the door!" (Getting people to go outside.)

"Not to making of THIS... oh, ick." I said that after a long string of words that just did not come out the way I wanted them to at all! After this, my child said, "Mom, you are hilarious. I love you! I am so glad you are my mom. Loving of you! " "Loving of you" is how I say "I love you" at times, so he sometimes says it that way to me.

"I will tell you about Amy and Ibby's book but not now because I am still to trying to making this work done."

"Loving of you!"

I should point out that I and my family often find this nonstandard communication enjoyable and fun. I once was concerned that I would accidentally start talking this way at work, and said that I would not talk like this anymore. On that day I was also using nonstandard writing and wrote this: "So one day got scared and said making myself not talking like that anymore. Person who heard was sad. Person liked the funny talking it was special to them but I said no, scared."

This is my "at home and not having so-called "correct words" speech. I do not use it in public because of a compartmentalization that is almost non-voluntary. I long to "slip up" and use this sort of speech everywhere so that I can "get it over with" and people will know "OK, she talks really weird" and get used to it and everyone will live happily ever after.

Back to "reality." It's not happening that way because I have a powerful internal self-censor that does not let anything slip out of my mouth that is not "perfect." The default level on this censor means that often I do not talk and can't get *any* words to come out. I don't hate myself, but my censor is looking out for me and does not want me to get in trouble. My censor is fear-based rather than self-hating, although that might not be much of an improvement. My self-censor seems to think I might have trouble keeping my employment if I looked at my employer and said "Writing of your this after the document making" or "Having of that piece of paper that is not another color but is a white paper because it's a document." The poor employer would be sure that I would not be competent to provide adequate documentation.

(After deciding to write anonymously, the written words are finally coming. What a struggle. Once I got to this paragraph, I happily said to my child, "Writing of this anonymously, can happen to it!" His response "Will anyone know it is you?" and I said "Maybe some will but can saying of what I need to say, more safe," upon which he said "You are a really good activist.")

If I ever did say the sky was green, and did not immediately correct myself for having chosen the wrong word, wait a second or two. Anyone reading this who thinks that I (or any Autistic who uses nonstandard speech) am now "much more dumb than I thought," I challenge you to rethink your assumptions. Again, no one reading this should assume that they will take over my communications for me as a form of "help," or that what I say when talking is not accurate. As I said above, I stop talking and switch to AAC (*if* the other communicator will permit it, which is often not the case), or drop speech altogether, if that is a danger for me. I will always do my own communicating, including any needed corrections. There is a huge difference between using/permitting/accepting/helping to obtain accommodations and jumping in and trying to speak *for* the person.

It is nice to not have to *try try try* all the time in my own home. Home is supposed to be where we can relax and be safe. I am fortunate in that I can use my non-thought-out speech here and be understood by my family. It is very relaxing. If I had a family member who did not understand (as in more distant relatives) I would switch to trying to speak "correctly" or being non-speaking.

To sum up my various types of AAC use: ASL; variety of non-paper boards that can be written on and then erased; dry erase board if at home near dry erase board; writing in both words and pictures (which can be worth at least a thousand words, and therefore cut down drastically on wait time when I am using non-speech-based methods!); scraps of paper, and whatever I can get my hands on. I have even written on tree bark, but that was just for fun.

I shuffle my communication methods and systems around depending on the situation. It is not a perfect system at times, but then, neither is the spoken word, even among non-autistics. Communication, for everyone, is always evolving, can always be improved upon, takes time and care to be successful.

❖ ❖ ❖

My Typed Voice
Alyssa Hillary

I am an Autistic person. My speech is usually and superficially *very* good. Superficially is a key word there. So is usually—not always. Both words make it harder for people to realize just how important typing is for my voice, both made it take longer than it should have to realize that sometimes I *can't* speak, and even when I technically can, maybe, just maybe, I *shouldn't* be using my mouth for speech. Not shouldn't as in not having anything that should be communicated: shouldn't as in mouth-sounds is the wrong way.

The reasons it took so long to realize that typing was a partial solution for my communication difficulties are assumptions society makes that need to be fixed, and frankly, the reasons it's only a partial solution are also problems in need of fixing: the problems I run into are much like those Mel Baggs ran into before me, in sier attempt at being a college student who does not always speak: Other people, sometimes people who claim to be experts in "people like me," make assumptions about my communication that are hilariously and potentially dangerously wrong.

In teacher training, we did personal introductions. I had not planned for these yet, and speech gave out on me during my introduction. Since I hadn't been expecting to need my laptop, it was closed, sleeping in my backpack, and therefore not available to explain what had happened at the rate I needed. (eSpeak on my laptop is the practical program for the professionally used word of speech generating device.) Instead, I located a pen and scribbled a short explanation on my folder, which I showed to the person running the training.

Everyone who saw me writing rather than speaking was actually fine. I was very lucky with that, and the fact that this is considered "lucky" rather than "meeting basic standards of decency" is one of the big problems I want to fix. That wasn't where the bad assumptions came in, not yet. It was where the question, "So what will you do if this happens in class?" got asked, and I had an answer. I still do have an answer, though I've only used it as a student and not yet as a teacher.

The problem was with a fellow teaching assistant, when I explained later what had happened. "You were shy," he said. "You were nervous," he said. (Not that he's unusual. He's just the example that came to mind, by way of being the most recent person to do this as I write.)

These were true statements. But they weren't the reason I lost speech. I'm shy, nervous, anxious, so often. If those things could break the mouth-sound kind of voice all on their own, I would never speak aloud with my mouth. Never. But most of the time, I can, and I do, and I can pass for having good speech by infodumping.

I am not the first to have faced this assumption. Mel dealt with this as well: sie can "remember one statement made by the local Autism Expert™: "Maybe we can help you reduce anxiety so you won't have to rely on your keyboard.[1]"" Like mine, sier speech isn't exactly *helped* by heaps of extra anxiety, but... it's not the main reason for speech to be less than ideal, and one of the main times when anxiety *is* a big deal? It's anxiety about what happens when typing is the better (or only) language-based choice that could work, but for reasons of other people, it's not an option.

The Autism Expert thinks life would be better if we didn't need to carry a keyboard around. A parent thinks the keyboard is encouragement not to get better at speaking with our mouths. A classmate decides we're just "faking it for attention." A *teacher* decides we're faking for attention, or simply does nothing while the classmates are bullies. Our parents, our teachers, everyone who's job it might be to help us learn to communicate more effectively assumes that if we can accomplish some things with oral speech some of the

---

1.   Baggs, Mel. "Autism, Speech, and Assistive Technology." 2000. Loud Hands: Autistic People, Speaking. Ed. Julia Bascom. Washington, DC: Autistic, 2012. 226-28. Print.

time, that must mean that we can accomplish all things with oral speech all of the time, and the idea of typing to communicate is never mentioned to us.

If we *do* find out, probably by chance, that some autistic people type to communicate because they never speak at all, we're told we're not like them because we can speak, nevermind that our speech isn't doing the things we need it to do for us.

But we're more like "those people" who type all the time, or who point to pictures, or who sign, or who use a mix of text and pictures, than most people would like to admit. We, who are often given the chance to prove that we have abilities, and having done so, are expected to hide our disabilities, are much more like the ones never allowed to prove their abilities than any binary system can handle. Disabled people can do things, and still be disabled. I can write, and sometimes speak, and be a student, and play sports, and have a social life, and type some of the time rather than speaking.

I can go to my university's computer club when communication via mouth-sounds aren't working for me, and I can plug my speakers into my laptop, and I can have my computer talk for me. People don't even always ask why I am speaking with my computer, once it's presented as something that simply exists. (Sometimes they ask. If they take issue with my answer, that's a sign that I don't want to be interacting with them, long term.) When I'm in Chinese class, I can have a classmate read what I typed aloud. (I still don't have good Chinese language text to speech, sadly.) I can e-mail the professor with what I typed during class, and my accommodations include "In terms of class participation, it counts like I said those things in class."

I have a voice in the world, and the consistency of my ability to express myself? It's not in spite of the fact that I (need to) type some of the time. It's *because* I choose typing over not communicating at all.

NonSpeakingNotSilent

autismdoggirl

I am 27 and I am an Autistic Adult, i Use AAC and communication apps for my primary form of communication. However I am not Nonverbal, or more accurately Growing up i was speech delayed, with a lot of work and time i became verbal, but now i rely on my communication device for almost all of my communication. Thus, I used to be verbal but I no longer speak. So i never know if i should refer to myself as non-speaking or nonverbal. I know that as you read this you might be a bit confused, so I will try to explain myself a bit better.

I first started using AAC when my interest was spiked as a way to help me communicate when I'm in sensory overload and can't physically speak. You see when I become overwhelmed scared or anxious I lose my ability to speak. So I first started using them to help when this would happen, little did I know how much of a difference AAC would make in my life,

Growing up I was delayed in many areas. One of those was speech, like many other autistic individuals. Why my speech was delayed i will never fully know or be able to say with 100 percent scientific accuracy. I can only tell you the reasons as I can remember them. For me speech was challenging for two main reasons. First I didn't think in spoken language. Rather my thoughts were not in spoken language, but rather in sensory experiences and thoughts. For me My first language was my senses, there has always been so much information coming into them, so much communication smells, tastes, sounds, sights, and textures all had information and meaning for me and they all shaped the way i understood and saw the world. This was is the major source of my memories

The second reason was because i had a lot of trouble getting the words in my head out through my mouth. For me there was a disconnect between my thoughts and my body. I would try to speak but the words would all come out blurred and meshed together and i would be missing words. as though half of my sentence got lost on the way out. So my sentences made very little sense and people often had a lot of trouble understanding me.

I remember before i could speak, when i was nonverbal and when i had little to no functional communication. I remember the frustration of not being able to get the words out, or the frustration when i would speak but only a small amount would come out. As well as the frustration of not having the words. Those this didn't really change as I became verbal.

Over time with a lot of speech and other therapies, as i said above, I became verbal. In fact I became very verbal. I could talk really well though i still had some difficulties that others who were paying attention might have been able to see and may have noticed. If anyone did notice they never mentioned it. most people remained happily unaware. Most people would have called my becoming verbal a success. They would have, and have, told me how well i was doing and how far I had come. However the truth is a lot more complicated than that. you see learning to talk and becoming verbal was not without it's consequences. The worst part was no one was even really aware of them.

The first was that even though I could speak, and i do so pretty well and had a very high verbal IQ, the truth is i was still struggling to communicate. Though no one realized it because i was verbal so they just assumed i could and was communicating just fine. They didn't realize i was just using chunk scripts to communicate. I remember not being able to explain or describe things. Everyone assumed since i could speak i would, and that i would be able to tell if anything bad happened to me. (They were wrong) Growing up I often acted out because I so desperately Wanted to be heard and understood. I would isolate myself or hyper focus even more on my special interest. In hopes that i might use it to connect with people and to gain more scripts I could use.. I also played my special interest a lot in similar attempts but i never understood the social norms of when to stop playing, For me it was a way of trying to communicate everything inside my head. however that didn't really work for me at all .

It was often extremely frustrating that no one realized i was struggling and wanting to be heard but couldn't get the words out. While I could talk very well i couldn't describe things well at all. I struggled to explain basic things, or be able to say my basic needs until they had surpassed my ability to handle them and i was about to explode. i don't know why I couldn't communicate these basic things but I couldn't see, to be able to get them into words and when I could I struggled to get them out. I was perfectly able to tell you all about cats as they were my special interest, but I couldn't get basic communication out, I struggled to describe the most basic of things. I could speak yes but I still couldn't communicate. Growing up i thought of myself as the bad kid because that's how many people saw me. I was hyper active and loud and had trouble sitting still and I stimmed a lot. I often acted out because i wasn't really able to communicate even though i could speak, though I was not trying to be bad. I couldn't tell the teacher if i was falling behind, or that i was having trouble understanding the material. I struggled a lot and did the best i could but i would often become stressed and overwhelmed so I would shut down. Which caused me to fall even further behind. So I stopped doing homework, it was way to frustrating and overwhelming for me. I couldn't just raise my hand and say i needed help, or ask anyone for help when i couldn't even manage to put into words what was wrong and what it was that i didn't understand about the materials so i ended up falling behind. I couldn't explain that sitting in class with the fluorescent lights was overwhelming or that the pencil was hurting my hand or that the teacher was going to fast. I couldn't tell them I hated writing when I would try to write one thing but my hands would write another or completely mess up the word. Which was likely related to disconnect which made speaking so hard.. So everyone saw me as the bad kid, and this is how i grew to view myself. I know now this was not the case. I wasn't a bad kid, I was a child desperately trying to be heard when everyone was assuming they were hearing all i needed or wanted to say.

The other consequence i hadn't even noticed at first, the more i became verbal the more i lost other skills and abilities to process my sensory input and the world around me.

As i became more and more verbal i became more and more detached from my environment and the world around me and from my sensory thinking. As i started to lose my sensory thinking some of my senses in fact began to feel a bit duller. however this did not stopped me from having sensory issues or becoming sensorially overloaded. i still have many sensory issues. they are just different now. i have the issues without the sensory connections I used to have. in losing the sensory thinking i lost a vital part of myself. The world has become even more frustrating, more confusing. I started losing my ability to think visually the way I used to. The more I use words for communication the more Ithought in words, the more the visuals fade away. I have become less able to process and safely navigate my environment. This resulted in me not noticing environmental hazards such as people, telephone poles and streets fast enough, often ending up with me walking or wandering into them. This has resulted in a few minor and even serious injuries.

Most of my ability to think, process and understand the world around me through my sense was lost. It had been taken away from me replaced with words. I can understand and formulate complex thoughts and ideas and even verbally explain many of them. Yet in-spite of this I can't give directions, I can't tell you where something is in the house. I struggle to tell a doctor what's wrong, how something hurts. And I struggle to communicate how I feel or to be able to explain what emotions i am having, when I'm upset, stressed, anxious or frustrated I can't speak as though something has cut the connection between my brain and at best I can only get noises out. This is why I first started using AAC to help when this would happen and give me a voice, but most people who knew me seemed to get even more upset with the AAC.

My brain can't seem to juggle understanding the world for what it is and using verbal communication at the same time. Temple once explained that with autism we don't have enough wiring to support all the parts of our brain and I do feel this is very true. When I had little to no speech all of the wires in my brain were linked to my sensory thinking. With therapy more and more wires were moved to verbal thinking and processing slowly overtime I began to lose a lot of my sensory thinking and it was being replaced with verbal thinking.

Some days verbal thinking is like a plague of a thousand voices screaming inside my head that I can't shut off. A jumbled mess of verbal thoughts with no clear point. As though my brain is spasming from the strain of thinking verbally and nothing I do will make them stop. unlike sensory thinking it does not feel natural (because it isn't) and I think for me it manifest differently than for those who are natural verbal thinkers. it is much more scattered and jumbled and relies heavily on a store of preset scripts that i use and break apart and reassemble. This makes conversation very difficult for me as I'm having to constantly do this and it is extremely exhausting.

this is a very stressful process for me and can even be painful. Constantly having to do this makes the world feel dead to me. And in-spite of the fact that I am verbal can speak and have some verbal thinking now, there is still so much I will never be able to communicate so much that remains trapped inside of me.

When I am verbal I often feel as if I'm stuck in a fog or haze and I have a lot of trouble focusing and remembering things. What's worse for me was losing a lot of the sensory thinking I had to have it replaced with verbal thought. For me to much verbal thought is extremely overloading and even painful. What's more the more I am verbal and think verbally, the more I lose my visual memory. This is not only upsetting but also impairing and it has made my faceblindness even harder, I had adapted to my face by recognizing them by their voice and scent, but also by what they were wearing, their hair and the context I knew them in. Loosing large amounts of visual memory for me meant I lost one of the major ways of how I recognize people as I needed to be able to remember the clothes they wore that day.

Becoming verbal caused me to lose my first language of sensory visual thinking, and a major part of who I was and my ability to properly perceive and understand the world around me. Loosing that ability made the world even more overwhelming and confusing, I spent many nights in tears feeling so lost and confused and overwhelmed. In learning to speak I traded the frustration of being non verbal, for not really being able to communicate and no one realizing it.

When I started using AAC for back up communication I didn't realize it would change my life, I had to go under medical procedures and I was unable to speak for a few weeks needing to rely on my AAC apps for all of my communication. Using AAC I began to better express myself, Communications became easier for me! I had to investigate this more so I decided to go a few months only using AAC to communicate

Over those few months I discovered using a communication device full time me enables to better manage my environment, navigate social situations and helps reduce the amount of over load I experience. This has also had many other surprising benefits. when I use my apps I to communicate I can and actually do communicate better. When I am verbal there is so much that remains trapped inside. Often I really want or need to say or tell someone something but the words just won't come out! This has been something I have struggled with my whole life! While using AAC I am able to communicate far more of what I need and want than I have ever been able to. Additionally I am able to draw better and bring far more detail into my drawings. I have become more aware of my environment and I am able to process visual information faster, thus I walk into things less and am more apt to notice if I am about to walk into a street. over all I am much happier. Using AAC and typing to communicate has also enabled me to better self advocate. The truth is for me, remaining nonverbal and using AAC to communicate has really helped me.

Deciding to give up being verbal and use AAC full time wasn't an easy choice! Even though it massively benefitted me I worried. I didn't want to offend or upset anyone, I feared I didn't have a right to full time AAC where I do have verbal skills. No matter how much it helped me. So I discussed this extensively with family, my fiancé and my therapist, I was surprised by some of the people who actually agreed with me and also /saw/ how this improved my life and told me that this was right for me and even told me it was ok and they supported me in this.

Yet I know there are many who would disapprove and be upset with me for this. Sometimes I worry that I don't have a right to stop speaking and to only use my AAC for communication, I worry being to speak I am obligated to do so and I know many people are likely to feel that way. So deep down I know some people will never understand me and with some It would never be accepted if they knew the truth. often I fear people will find out I used to be verbal and they will be upset and they won't understand. That really scares me and breaks my heart! I'm am not faking and this really is something I really need. I may have been verbal but I couldn't communicate not like I can now!

In the end I need to do what is right for me, using the AAC apps for my predominant form of communication and only speaking rarely with those I am close to has really changed my life. it has restored some of what I have lost and as time goes on more of what I have lost is returning. I am happier, healthier and I am communicating. I have been able to actually self advocate for the first time in my life. I can better manage my own environment with my visual processing improving I am able to navigate and get around safer and I am getting lost less. I'm even beginning to recognize people a bit better. This was not an easy choice, but it has been life changing and it is what Is best for me so I will continue using my AAC full time. I know there will always be people who will disapprove and who will think poorly of me because of this, however their approval or disapproval will not change what is right for me. I have been blessed with a few close friends, a fiancé and a few wonderful family members who know this is what I need for me. and they understand and support me in this and for that I am truly grateful! They love and accept me how I am and for who I am, I could never begin to thank them enough for that or express to them how much that really means to me!

I hope this has helped you to understand some and to realize just because someone is verbal and seems to talk well it doesn't mean they don't struggle or severe communication issues. If you take only one thing from this let it be that There are more reasons for needing AAC then just being unable to speak. there are many more this is mine Each of us using AAC and typing to communicate has a voice, deserve to be heard and respected. We are not alone!

❖ ❖ ❖

Notes on Not Speaking
Bridget Allen

For Confused Helpers: Clarification on Why I Need to Type

I love words. Words as toys, words as art, words as a distillation, a snapshot of what was.

I hate words.

Words are pale, small, and imprecise.

In order for you to understand how complex the journey to arrive at words is for me, I need to use words.

It feels unfair.

#

In the beginning there are thoughts. Thoughts are vibrant or muted. They are color. They make sense internally, but they have no words. Thoughts can be distilled into metaphor, tangible images and sequences. Then begins the work of describing the metaphor with words. I become the narrator of my mind. If I'm lucky, a direct description of the metaphor will suffice. More often, I'll need to break down the symbolism of the metaphor into simple, descriptive language. Once I have that boiled down to a sentence or two, I can play it repeatedly inside my head so it feels comfortable as a thing I can verbalize, much like reading words from a book.

That is work.

It's exhausting, and there is a limit to how long I can keep it up. Extended speaking is like running a marathon. I need time, care, and preparation in order to perform. Even world caliber marathon runners only run two or three marathons a year.

#

When I cannot speak, it is because I cannot speak. Don't make this into something else. I am not shy. I am not too upset to speak. Please do not tell me to calm down. My emotional distress and my ability to verbalize are not linked. Do not imply that if I could stop being overly emotional I would suddenly be able to communicate in a manner that fits in your comfort zone. My emotions play into my speaking only in that any complicated task is more difficult to carry out when under duress. That's a fairly universal human experience.

Vocalization is not an automatic process for me. You underestimate the significance of this. No, really. Don't pretend you understand. Don't insist it's the same for you. I know you think about the words you say. I know sometimes you misspeak, but you need not actively think about how to speak or how to make the words come out as something others understand. You do not have to keep vigilant attention to volume lest you spend a mountain of energy turning pictures into words only to find you spoke them all as an inaudible subvocalization.

#

I can walk. Walking is an automatic process. A bad spine and arthritis often make walking painful. I may stumble because I have little feeling in my feet. Nerve damage may make my legs buckle and cause me to fall. Poor proprioception may cause me to run into a door frame or table. Still, if I want to walk into the kitchen for a cup of coffee, I do not have to consciously think about moving my left leg forward, placing weight on my left foot, pushing off from my left foot while moving my right leg forward, etc. Those movements are automatic. If I had to make a conscious effort to think through all those actions in order to take a single step, I would have no way to think about anything else and still move. It would be overwhelming. I certainly could walk under those circumstances, but doing so would be a significant drain on my quality of life.

#

My verbalization is a finite resource. If I use too much of it, I will run out. Because the FCC does not allow the use of tty/ttd technology for my disability, it is critical I keep some reserve in case an emergency requires I call 911. Gauging my verbal stamina, while based on decades of experience, is still only a guess. I'm going to err on the side of caution because anything less would be irresponsible.

When I vocalize for you, I am sacrificing my quality of life to do so. Given that, I have a right to make damn sure it's worth my while. You do not have a right to demand I vocalize any time I can. I do not owe you this very limited resource simply to mollify or make myself less of an inconvenience. If I am not worth the minor effort on your part to communicate with me in a way that preserves my safety and well being, you are not worth the major effort on my part to do otherwise.

#

I am well aware there is wonderful AAC technology available. I have a tablet, and I count on it for help with communication, sensory regulation, and executive function. Text-to-speech software has been wonderful for many, but not for me. The social pressure to shoehorn it into my repertoire was intense. Each person who broaches the subject of text-to-speech does so as if they are imparting information I had never heard before. I understand why you want my typing to be text-to-speech. It appeals to you because it means I am communicating in your language. I tried to adapt, to change. I tried to meet you where you are, but I simply cannot manage.

In the multi-step process of converting thoughts to words, sometimes when those words come back into my ears as I speak them, the process grinds to a halt. The entirety of my words unspoken vanish. Gone. It's all gone. One phrase in, and my ability to converse, even by typing is lost. When my words come back filtered through an electronic device, the process breaks down every time. I have practiced alone, away from the pressure to converse. I hoped against hope that I could acclimate myself, but that one sentence pouring out my iPad in someone else's voice breaks the delicate chain of thoughts to words without fail. Then I'm isolated, unable to communicate in any manner. It's frightening beyond what you imagine.

The best text-to-speech technology can ever offer me is a one-line script.

#

With the best of intentions, they taught me to script. For ten years of my childhood, the family members I trusted most honed my false communications. Hour upon hour nibbling homemade divinity, sipping tea, and practicing phrases designed to set others at ease.

My scripts sound natural and border on elegant. Layer enough scripts on top of each other and the results are snippets of performance art in which I play the part of someone warm and charming. All my scripts are scripts of compliance. There is no room for me in those words. Perhaps they assumed I would figure it out. Perhaps they meant to teach me how to say no when I got older, but before I got older, they were all gone. Instead, all that

"But, of course,"
"Why, certainly,"
"I'd love to,"
"It's not a problem," and
"I'd be more than happy to,"
bought me was a sea of debt, sacrificed health, and unbidden touching. Only in the written word can I protect myself. When they tried to lock me away, I find it no coincidence that the first thing they took from me was my notebooks and pens.

Scripting is a pale imitation of real communication. It is a dangerous activity because the words that fall out of my mouth are always believed over any other communication. No matter how many times I shook my head no, screamed without volume, shoved, and scratched, and pushed away, it was nothing in the face of witnesses who heard me say, "Thank you so much," for the ride home.

So I will keep my typed words, my real words. I tried to find a way to fit into your world of constant chatter, and no matter how hard I tried, it was never good enough. In my typed words, I matter. Me as I actually am, not as a facsimile designed to please others. Communication is human, but communication is gloriously complex. It is much more than only speech, it is more than words. It is truth, and truth cannot be bridled by transitory societal standards.

Overload
Lydia Wayman

Every morning, I take in a gulp of air and shut my eyes tight before I plunge beneath the surface.

One, two, three...

I count not seconds or minutes, but hours.

Starved of air, short-circuiting synapses spark and tingle.
Four, five, six...

Unintelligible flashes, ratcheting crashes pierce my consciousness,

Like trying to watch TV while the radio plays and fire ants climb my legs, every eighth one biting my skin.

Seven, eight, nine…

Now disoriented in the murky water,

I reach for the worry stone in my pocket.

Ten!

I cannot break the surface fast enough.

I yank the wool sweater off. My weighted blanket engulfs my body, the deep pressure reaching each misfiring neuron.

Breathe.

Note: For me, loss of speech very much stems from sensory overload; this poem describe the overload that results in losing speech and explains how an overwhelmed body and brain are so all-encompassing that speech is no longer possible.

❖ ❖ ❖

Itsa Crying Shame - Severely Gifted
P. Allen

On a scale of one to ten
Eleven wouldnt do u justice
But no-one was counting then
Who was taking down scores ,
Only noticing the flaws
When the rules of the game changed
As the world just wants a little more
From a child whose just growing

Itsa a long road figuring out the puzzle

Unravel the paths, threads,dreads

Shake off the self imposed muzzle

With a road map a sketch on a tissue

Melted away decades ago

All that remains is a visual

So i now connect the dots, late at night

Line up past mistakes by laptop lite

Learn about myselves in 3,4,5,D

Theoretically weaving,

Looking for potential still missing

You always knew it wouldnt be easy

When u were so young , didnt have a say

Life felt like a continual test ,

So you just pushed on and prayed

Yeah itsa shame

Itsa yes and a no ,

But that was back in the day

There u go.. off again ..off i go

Into the beautiful blue horizon

The one i created a longtime ago

To retreat into ,

To run or fly away into

As its the only one i know

Maybe we're on our own

But guided by angels

With minds like our own,

But we're not alone

I want u to know .

Its little understood that feeling inside....

Thats what makes me cry....

But its ok

Its ok ....cos im alive...we're still alive.

Creative Writing

Paul Hope Park

[**Editorial note:** This was part of an exercise and the text in italic are the instructions given to Paul, who then typed his views and responses.]

CREATIVE WRITING: Reflect on the Renaissance; a celebration of art, science and philosophy from the 14th through 16th centuries. Humanistic scientific theory and religious reverence were often simultaneously expressed through artistic endeavors. You have commissioned a modern day artist to paint the ceiling of your bedroom. Describe elements that would be represented. People, Places, Things, Personal Interests, Representations of Literature, Music, Sports, Landmarks in your Neighborhood.... Anything that you would want to celebrate and commemorate on your ceiling for all times!

Paul wrote — I WOULD LOVE TO PAINT THE CEILING OF MY BEDROOM. I WOULD MAKE IT MY VERY OWN MASTERPIECE. IT WOULD REPRESENT EVERYTHING IMPORTANT TO ME. FIRST IT WOULD SHOW MY LOVE FOR MY MOTHER. SHE IS MY ENTIRE MOTIVATION TO BE A BETTER PERSON. NEXT I WOULD PAINT THE JOY I FEEL FROM BEING ABLE TO COMMUNICATE ON THE LETTER BOARD. I WOULD INCLUDE ALL THE LOVE I FEEL FOR THE MANY SPECIAL PEOPLE WHO GUIDE MY WAY THROUGH THIS LIFE WITH SUCH DEDICATION. I WOULD REPRESENT MY INTEREST IN SPORTS BY PAINTING BRUSH STROKES THAT SHOW SKATING, HOCKEY, DIVING, AND RUNNING. I WOULD INCLUDE PAINTING OF SOME THINGS THAT I ENJOY LIKE PLAYING PIANO, PRAYING, HANGING OUT WITH FRIENDS AND TIME TO MYSELF. DO NOT THINK THAT I HAVE FORGOTTEN NATURE AND ALL THE BEAUTIFUL THINGS THAT GOD HAS MADE. I WOULD LIKE TO WAKE UP EVERY MORNING AND SEE THESE REMINDERS OF ALL VERY SPECIAL GIFTS IN MY LIFE, TREASURED PEOPLE, AND UNUSUAL GLORY FROM GOD. THE END.

CREATIVE WRITING:*Paul's speech therapist asked after a lesson on The Seven Wonders of the World. She asked — The Seven Wonders of the World was written as a tour guide. Create your own Seven Wonders tour guide!*

Paul wrote — MY SEVEN WONDERS TOUR GUIDE IS FOR LIFE. WHEN YOU ARE A BABY WONDER HOW YOU WERE MADE AND WHAT YOUR LIFE WILL BE LIKE. WHEN YOU ARE SMALL, WONDER HOW THE WORLD WORKS. WHEN YOU BECOME A TEENAGER, WONDER HOW THE WORLD SEES YOU. WHEN YOU FINALLY BECOME AN ADULT WONDER HOW YOU CAN CHANGE THE WORLD. WHEN YOU ARE A PARENT, WONDER HOW YOU CAN TEACH YOUR CHILD ABOUT THE WORLD. WHEN YOU ARE OLD WONDER HOW YOU AFFECTED THE WORLD. WHEN YOU ARE DYING, WONDER HOW THE WORLD WILL REMEMBER YOU.

3. Paul's speech therapist asked after a lesson about Rosh Hashanah — If you were celebrating Rosh Hashanah and reflecting on your year, good and bad, what would your reflections be?

Paul wrote — I would say this has been an amazing year! Because I can now communicate through RPM. This has changed my life forever. My whole way of living has gone in a new happier trajectory. Going forward, I feel there is nothing I cannot do.

Nonspeaking (at times) Autistic Makes Video

*Paula
C. Durbin-
Westby*

I am not a completely nonspeaking Autistic, of course. Many people have seen me speak and some do not even know that I lose speech at times. My loss of speech is temporary, and can last a few seconds to a few hours or the good part of a day. Sometimes it really *is* the *good part* of the day, as I often find talking to be exhausting and it's nice to not have to do it, even if it is because I temporarily *can't* do it.

The following short video clip is part of what is going to be a longer video. I have about 5 or 6 of the segments made, but need to get to a much faster

Internet connection to upload them, and need some more time to edit it all into one video. Here's for starters. This one was made today, when I was not able to speak.

For me, not being able to speak does not always coincide with "social anxiety." I was at home, with only the dogs around. No social anxiety. I also was a bit tired all day because I had insomnia the night before, which made me less likely to be able to talk. I only have so much energy. Various things precipitate my not being able to speak: being tired, being overloaded, trying to talk when other people are talking too fast over me, reading or seeing something disturbing. Or, in the case of yesterday, because I was not speaking to anyone but working at the computer, I was "not used to talking anymore" and so had trouble getting started again. It does not take more than half a day of not talking for whatever reason before I need to sort of urge myself to take it up again.

Not being able to speak is very much like, and perhaps exactly like, having an epidural and not being able to wiggle your toe because you are numb from the waist down. I had an epidural once. I tried to wiggle my toe. I tried a lot. It was an experiment! A doctor saw me and said "Cut it out!" "Cut what out?" "You're trying to wiggle your toe." (How could he tell?!) He said that attempting to wiggle my toe was making all the nerves fire that led from my brain to my toe, only nothing was going to happen. He explained that I was wasting precious physical energy that I would need for recovery (kidney stone procedure). About 5 years ago I tried another experiment—to talk when I could not. I tried to force myself—mind over matter!—and had that same feeling. It's like the nerves that go from my brain to my mouth have disconnected, temporarily.

Regarding the analogy to an epidural. The analogy is more than a simple comparison. The epidural kept me from being able to wiggle my toe, even though all the neurons were firing. I felt physically exhausted, even though nothing had moved! And, the day I did the two-hour experiment (which is not discussed in this video clip) to try to make myself talk, I felt that same feeling and thought "I have had this before..." and remembered the epidural. Probably the process is not exactly the same, but for me (and this might not apply to anyone else, but probably does), it *was* the same experiece and feeling, trying to do something I could not physically do, and being exhausted from trying. I will go into this in more detail in my next few videos (have 5-6 clips).

I will write more in the coming few days and weeks. I have been wanting to make one of these for a long time but I had to have a time when I could not talk AND I wanted to make a video AND I remembered to do it AND I was not having a bad hair day. ;)

(One clarification: At the part when the text says "I guess I should try harder" and then I say "That makes me sad," I don't mean sad about not speaking. I mean sad about people saying "Oh, you should just try harder" about things that people can't do, or can't do as easily as others, and especially when children with disabilities hear that.)

TRANSCRIPT:
(In general there is mostly silence, sort of white noise in the background most of the time. The scritching sounds are me writing with a black magic marker on sheets of paper.)

First sheet of paper:
"OK, right now? I am not able to talk. I am going to try a little experiment. Let's see if I can make myself talk."
Then it shows me trying to talk. I am really trying to even move my mouth but I am not able to do it much. So then I write a note (scritching sounds). I am smiling while I am writing this. Then I try once more to make some sounds:
"I can't even move my mouth! I thought I would do that...." (means I thought I would be able to move my mouth and get started on talking.) Then I am smiling while I write the next one:
"I am probably not trying hard enough."
But then, that makes me start to look sad, on the video. I write another piece of paper:
"That was supposed to be a joke, but it makes me sad. :("
Then I add to that:
"Especially for KIDS." And I do not look very happy at all.
My last piece of paper says:
"OK, this is SO not working. ttyl. (Type to ya later.)
Then I smile a little bit and wave goodbye.

❖ ❖ ❖

I Am Meaningful
Philip Reyes

I am somebody.
I am your son.
I am a brother.
I am a cousin.
I am a student.

One day I can be an educator,
A rounded person to imitate.
I can be a worker,
Make a really good living.
I can be a loving friend,
Someone to confide in.

I am autistic, but I am learning I am much more.
I am me and I like me a lot.

❖ ❖ ❖

Typing
Philip Reyes

I want to type well because it is utilised in many situations. The real world uses the typed word all the time, for we come to communicate by texts, Facebook, and emails. I am now a part of the digital age.

The reality is I was special to learn to type. Mom really pushed me to practice really hard everyday. Typing is very hard. I need to concentrate so hard placing my finger on the right keys. I undermine typing every time I tense up. Tension comes from going to stoop your self down to destructive stims. My title undermining stims are having to move my body and really hurling myself on the ground. Not remembering the reason I wanted to pour my total emotions out is frustrating. I truly irritate myself when I really lose control of myself. I have such a hard time focusing on what I want to say. I need someone to keep me focused to get the right word out and initiate my movement in purposeful ways. To type my real thinking I need a trusted person to encourage me through the reaching out of my words. I think I am improving everyday with practice.

Typing is having a voice with your really good friends writing letters and texts. Typing is connecting with the world. Typing is touching interested people understanding autism. Typing is God's gift to me.

❖ ❖ ❖

Typing to Talk is Healing
Philip Reyes

I type to talk. Without typing I have no voice to tell you I am smart. I spell my thoughts because I cannot speak with my mouth. Thoughts remain imprisoned in my mind escaping only through my finger on a letterboard or keyboard. I tell of my experiences of being autistic in my writing and blog. Without typing I am misunderstood as retarded and unteachable. You cannot tell from my exterior that I am following everything you say. Understanding comes easy to me. You treat people how they withstand the environment without autism. In my experience, autism traps me in a realm where I am not in control of my actions. The tantrums I have result from frustrations I have over my mind being unable to hold my body in service to my desire to use my body appropriately. I may want to place a pencil to paper to draw a picture, but my hand refuses to grasp and it each time moves purposelessly. I really have to work hard to teach myself skills. The truth is my intelligence is profoundly masked by autism. Typing your thoughts with a trusted partner is healing to a quiet life in which there is no real communication. I eagerly type so I can be known by others. My true self is revealed in my typed words. The reason I type is life that I love is hearing how you think and expressing how I think too. To type is freedom to my soul. You people who can talk have no idea the pain I have not speaking. It is the torment of the soul for no one to know you. I am much happier now that I can type.

❖ ❖ ❖

FRIENDSHIP
Quinn Partridge

When I plan my life I want to have lots of friends. I want people to like me. Just know it is my great hope to get married. But please understand how hard it is.

Please know I hope to be more independent. I need help with just about everything. I really get frustrated if my friends have other things to do. Some people get me mad. They look the other way if I come near them. I need to have better social skills. Help me behave better.

People blame me if I do bad things. I nicely try to be good, but know that I love living on my own. Just see how much I am learning. I have learned pretty much about gardening. I have learned better as how to do laundry. Just know I like going places with my friends.

I like being with people, mostly I like girls. They seem like they know I am intelligent. People give my mom good news about places to go. Olivia is my best friend. Emma is my next best friend.

Not being able to talk makes my life very frustrating. Having my letter board has changed my life. My best friends are very patient. They just know I need to get my ideas spelled out.

I need help to just be happy going new places. I like it best if lots of kids go places but my friends are busy. Maybe they like time to be on their own.

People need to know I am very smart. I like living on my own. Please know I need lots of help so I can communicate. Good friends believe in my intelligence.

"typer interrupted"
Rick Maives

"typer interrupted"

words typed last forever
words spoken come and go
the typer tells of years of frustration

the talker has the advantage of really saying whatever and being believed.
the truth is typers think through their words
talkers don't have the same commitment
to their words
our truth is our freedom

"thoughts to free thinking"

the years of silence made me a more introspective mind. i was forever hearing all. there are things i know that i wish i did not. the fly on the wall has hugh responsibility to listen and keep others secrets. this responsibility is something i took seriously.

i have great expectation to be the silent keeper for good of all.

this knowledge took a toll on my heart.

i can try for others well being to remain silent. self expression is a right for everyone. my daily typing and my art help me to be not only seen but valued as a person of substance. the world is missing out when they dismiss those of us who do not use the spoken word to communicate. what we have to say is worth the time and patience necessary to hear us. slow down and really hear our voices. we are an untapped resource of ideas.

Ron's writing

Ron Giri

1. "The Unsure Wolf"

One day a wolf forgot what he liked to eat. So he had no idea what to do. He decided to try many types of food. He ate lamb curry and rice. It was very hot and spicy. Then he ran into a pond and jumped into it to cool himself down. He did not know how to swim. So he drowned and died.

Morale: Never try something that you are unsure of.

2. "Father"

Fill me with love
And kindness
To help me all the time
Heart of gold
Even when we are naughty
Remain in my life forever

3. Summer

Sun shining brightly
Umbrellas inside
More people going out
Many children playing
Everywhere flowers blossoming
Roses smelling sweet and nice

❖ ❖ ❖

Solitary Confinement
Roy Bedward

If you understood how important it is to be able to communicate you would never have the heart to doubt fc. Please try to understand how it matters more than anything to us. This is the main message of my life.

This is like being trapped your whole life then the door to your cage opens and you are no longer in solitary confinement. Imagine being in solitary confinement before you even know there is such a thing as communicating. Then imagine being able to share your thoughts. Then imagine going back to solitary if you cannot type on your own. That happens to me every day. The cage is open and then it is slammed shut. It is not easy to go from freedom to solitary.

Tasting freedom makes the solitary all the worse. If you could understand that you would be my friend for life. How can others think solitary confinement is ok?

How does it feel to be in solitary? Let me tell you. It is the most lonely thing you can imagine. The cell has windows so you can see everyone but you cannot help yourself to any words to even just say hello. You are nothing more than an animal in the zoo.

You are pleasing to no one and hated by the others. People make faces but do not really see you. They only see a trapped animal.

Going to the limits of your own ability is the thing that matters most. Just think about how much is lost or wasted by not having the things we need. Those things are the difference between life and living death. Just imagine every little baby that is born never being hungry for food for other things that it needs. It would grow in a way that we cannot even imagine. It would not ever have to prove its worth but would have its worth by being born.

Please understand the importance of using words to communicate. It is the most important thing of all. If i could not use words even part of the time it would be much harder to control myself. I need the reminder that i am human after all. Without words it is easy to forget that fact. Being human in my own mind is the first step to being seen as human by others.

Please understand too that if I cannot use words then my only recourse is behavior. And we all know that can sometimes turn out in unfortunate ways. Please see my behavior as the desperate failings of a man with no options. If I had words all the time the behavior would not be necessary. As it is now, I only use behavior when things are intolerable or otherwise impossible.

I need to say one more thing about this. If ever the time comes to help others understand typing I will be the first in line to do my part. It is my mission in life. I think you are my test audience.

❖ ❖ ❖

The Song of Life Unfolding

Sparrow Rose Jones

The other day, some of my friends and I were discussing the importance of words and meaning and context. It turns out, though, that what we were really discussing was communication. In most humans, so much communication happens through words that we can forget that the communication is more important than the words. One thing we all noticed about words and communication was how they affect attention, awareness, and understanding.

Because it took so long for me to begin communicating about communicating, I had no meaning or context when I first began to lose speech. I didn't have that attention, awareness, and understanding that comes from putting life events in their correct context. I don't remember how old I was when I first noticed that I sometimes lost the ability to speak, but my memories go back to age two and it was before I started pre-school, so somewhere between age two and four is when I first noticed that sometimes it was easy to make words with my mouth but sometimes the words wouldn't happen. My mother gave me the only context I was to have for years.

I needed something and I couldn't make the words, so I pointed and tried to make the right sounds. "Use your words," my mother said. "I know you can talk," she reminded me. "I don't respond to grunts," she admonished.

I've since seen these sorts of responses suggested in parenting books. They might be good responses for developing children with no neurological issues. They are probably just right as gentle nudges for most children. For me, they were frustrating because I couldn't get my needs met, even when it was clear that my requests were understood. For me, they were frightening. A child is relatively helpless and has needs for shelter, for relief of hunger and thirst, for love and acceptance. These are needs that the child looks to others to fill. When a child can't get their needs met, there is frustration and fear. When a child asks to have their needs met and that request is understood but rejected, there is anger and confusion.

My communication difficulties were paradoxically compounded by my facility with communication. When I can talk, boy do I ever talk. When the words are coming out of my mouth, they flow like water, threatening to drown the listener. "I know you can talk." Oh, yes, I sure can. Sometimes. Many of my difficulties are like that: intermittent. Because I passed my hearing test, I was "obviously" choosing to ignore what people said. Because I could walk and run and play, I was "obviously" making my muscles go floppy intentionally from laziness or an urge to frustrate others, and because I could speak, I was "obviously" being lazy when I didn't use my words. Like so many other aspects of who and how I am, these early lessons about me were so powerful that they erased my own understanding of myself. I wasn't skilled enough with self-advocacy to explain what was really happening, so the explanations that others laid upon me were enforced, reinforced, and accepted by everyone, including the one person who knew better: me. As it turns out, there were professionals who attempted to diagnose me in childhood but my mother refused to allow it. She said she couldn't see it. To her, it looked like she had a child who was emotionally troubled, naughty, or lazy; not a disabled child who struggled honestly. That mislabeling affected my self-perception for decades.

Through the years, I continued to lose the ability to speak on a regular basis. Because I had never been allowed to understand that there was a neurological cause, I foraged for explanations. I was shy. I was anxious. I was stupid. Sadly, that was the one I settled into the easiest: that I was stupid and sometimes couldn't talk because I had nothing worth saying. sadly, this is an explanation so much of the world loves. But I am not stupid. And I do have important things to say. As the developer of facilitated communication, Dr. Rosemary Crossley said, "not being able to speak is not the same as having nothing to say."

Most of my life, my reaction to losing my voice was to hide. I felt stupid, exposed, at risk. How could I get my needs met with no voice? How could I protect myself from danger with no voice? I was frightened and ashamed, so I hid. For years, I hid whenever I couldn't speak. Since I could talk sometimes, I couldn't bear to let people know there were other times when I couldn't. I felt I was facing an impossible choice between letting people believe I really could speak but was stubbornly and strangely choosing not to or helping them understand that I really couldn't speak, only to be judged as deficient for it.

Learning that I am Autistic began to undo some of the years of damage to my sense of self. I began to understand that I am not a tragically flawed "normal" person but an Autistic person of crystalline beauty, different from most around me, but competent, capable, valuable, and worthy. But still, I struggled with how to handle those times when I cannot speak. In fact, I shouldn't say "struggled" because it isn't something that has ended. I wrote this essay in the last two days of the call for submissions because it took me months to believe I had any business writing for this anthology. It took me months to convince myself that there was any chance this essay might be accepted. It took me months to feel brave enough to believe that I would not be insulting the struggles of others by writing this.

I have the ability to speak sometimes. I have the privilege of being mainly judged for those times when I am speaking. I have the privilege of being able to hide when I cannot speak, at least most of the time, because there are other times when I can speak, other times when I can show myself and get my needs mostly met, and be heard by others, and be automatically viewed as competent. What finally convinced me to write this essay? I am in the middle of a stretch of not-speaking. It started two Mondays ago. It's been going on for more than a week. I have things I need to do but can't because I'm unable to make a phone call right now and people hang up on me when I try to call them using my AAC device. I am doing better than I used to—I left the house a couple of times during this period of being unvoiced, something I never would have done in the past.

It took another episode of being unvoiced to make my typed voice loud enough to potentially carry all the way into this anthology. If you are reading this, my voice was loud enough to be heard this time.

Why am I so timid about speech and typing? I have seen this fear take myriad forms in other people—the fear of not being "disabled enough to deserve support." Because I can speak sometimes, I fear that I don't deserve support when I can't. I fear that my seeking support is, in some way, taking away from those who are not-speaking full-time. It's a good thing that fear isn't required to make logical sense because this one doesn't. Supports are not a zero sum game. The supports I get do not take away from someone else's supports. I think it may be the opposite: the more those of us who need them seek and receive supports, the more we boldly access supports while others are watching, the more we treat supports as a natural thing that we deserve to have, the more we and those like us will be able to get supported in our needs. Getting and using supports normalizes them. It creates more access, not less.

A real turning point for me in feeling permitted to use AAC to help me when I am unable to speak came when I read some essays by Mel Baggs in hir blog "Ballasexistenz." Sie wrote that alternative communication is "not just for people who absolutely can't ever speak," and sie said that sie has "run into too many people lately who desperately need something like this, but are afraid to use it because they don't fit the popular image of someone who needs a communication device. Some of them have even been told that it's horrible or disrespectful of them to even consider using a communication device. But my position on it is that having the most effective communication method possible can result in better emotional and physical health, in some situations it can even save lives."

Reading that was a great relief for me. Mel wrote, "If something like this can make your life better, for any reason at all. Whether you can't ever speak, can only sometimes speak, can only speak about certain topics, can speak but it isn't what you mean, can speak but typing or using picture icons works better or uses fewer mental resources. Or anything else like that. Do whatever works best for you, and screw anyone who tells you different." This became my new rallying cry: I will do what works best for me and screw anyone who tells me differently!

My first attempt at typing when I couldn't speak did not go so well, however.

I still felt like I couldn't ask for help in acquiring the tools to communicate effectively. I still struggled with feeling unworthy. So I tried to figure out what I could use. I became unvoiced and needed to go to class and had nothing that could replicate speech. So I went in to my small seminar class with a laptop computer, opened to a text program. I naïvely thought that typing my words would work in the small class of only 4 students. I indicated to the professor that I couldn't speak that day. He said, "oh, you have laryngitis" and I just let that assumption sit. I was trembling with nervousness at my boldness and in no place to challenge assumptions. I was just hoping I could get through the day.

I couldn't.

First, I was unable to participate in the conversation, because no one was willing to stop and read what I had written, even though I was willing to pass the laptop around for everyone to see. My participation was clunky and it slowed down the flow of conversation. I could have been sharing the most brilliant ideas in academia (I assure you, I wasn't) and no one would have cared. I tried to enlist my seat mate to read my words for me. He indicated that he would, but the first time I handed him words to read, he pretended to read them but instead made some embarrassing sexual comments, pretending that it was what I had really written. Angry and ashamed, I packed up my books and left class.

That was my last time trying to communicate while unvoiced for a long time.

Not so long after that, I re-visited a childhood interest and began to learn ASL (American Sign Language) in earnest. I had been very interested in ASL as a pre-teen, but without anyone to communicate with, I learned little and remembered even less. It was a source of great joy to me when I realized that the "whatever it is" that sometimes stops the words from coming out of my mouth does not silence my hands. I joined the ASL club on campus and made some friends. My signing, while improving daily, was still rudimentary when I realized that I had friends with whom I could communicate even when I was unvoiced and whom I could understand, even in the noisy environments that conspire with my CAPD (central auditory processing disorder) to convert spoken language to meaningless garble. I will always love ASL for the way it opened up my options for communication, for the new friends it brought to me, and for its exuberant beauty and joy.

But ASL has one trait that made it only a partial solution for my communication difficulties—it's not English. I love ASL and continue to learn and use it every day, but it is a separate language and so it opened the door into a different culture. I love Deaf culture so much, but ASL didn't open most of the doors that have been closed to me most of my life. Knowing enough ASL to get my basic needs met has helped me at the hospital and doctor's office and I am sure it would help me in an airport. But usually no one at the grocery or laundromat understands ASL. It is a foreign language to most Americans. I love it, but I needed more ways to communicate when unvoiced.

Every so often, I shyly mentioned my intermittent difficulties with communication and one day a friend unexpectedly stepped in to help me get set up with a real AAC! I now use an app called Verbally on an iPad mini. I have a little bluetooth speaker because the iPad is not very loud and I have an Apple bluetooth keyboard for times when I want to have a full conversation with someone, because typing on a screen is good for shorter messages but gets exhausting when there are longer things to say.

I love my AAC device! I still struggle with my feelings, but I struggle so much less with communication now. There are still a few people who don't react well when I am unvoiced, but the people who love me are happy for me. I used to hide from the world when I was unvoiced, but this latest episode that I find myself in the middle of has been an affirmation of personal power. I have left my house for groceries. I have had conversations with the person I am dating. I have a voice! I am heard! I can get my needs met! I feel valued and wanted, not brushed aside and ignored. Having a reliable way to communicate when my voice goes away has changed my life; I am blossoming.

And I can't help thinking about those of my brothers and sisters who are always non-speaking. If being able to type when I can't speak part-time has been such a powerful force for good in my life, how much more revolutionary must it be in the lives of those who are able to type when they can't speak full-time? Anne McDonald, one of the first people to use facilitated communication, wrote that "crushing the personalities of speechless individuals is very easy: just make it impossible for them to communicate freely." I have gotten repeated tastes of what it feels like to be crushed that way. There are some who have a full menu of little but that crushing oppression. I am, bit by bit, more open about my intermittent speech difficulties and more open about using my AAC instead of hiding from the world and I hope that it means I am one more person helping to build a world where alternate means of communication are normalized and available for everyone who needs them.

Communication is a fundamental human right and being allowed to communicate in a language that is comfortable and accessible—typing, ASL, PECS, facilitated communication, Bliss, or whatever works for a person—is of paramount importance. When a person's attempts to communicate are brushed aside or denied to them, a very serious crime has been committed. People need to communicate and denying that need is criminal. As my friends and I observed the other day, communication affects attention, awareness, and understanding. But more than that, communication affects how we feel about being human—whether we feel included or shut out from participating in the community that surrounds us. It is so important that we make sure the channels of communication are kept open for everyone, through whatever means each of us needs, without shame or guilt, without agendas that privilege speech as more important than communication. Those who can speak sometimes should not be discouraged from typing to communicate as needed. Even those who can always make words with their mouths often find typing a more eloquent and less stressful means of communicating than speech. No one should feel that they have to prove they are "disabled enough" to deserve the supports that will make their lives easier, happier, and more productive.

Increasing my ability to communicate with others has filled me with so much hope and joy. I want everyone to feel that way. I want everyone to be heard. Typed voices are a celebration of communication and connection. Listen to them and rejoice. The clicking of the keyboard is the song of life unfolding.

❖ ❖ ❖

Story
Ethan

My life is not interesting so my mom made me learn RPM. Suddenly, life, quiet was interesting. I got spelling. My mom, my dad, grandma, and sister find me nice going. My sad days are over. Typing made me more like everyone. To talk is happy for some. Happy to some is to type.More happy to my giving mom.

The end

The World through my Hands
Lydia Wayman

Andante

My spirit finds rest in church,

My focus finds challenge.

So, I bring a bracelet with beads.

I rhythmically spin them to the pace of the sermon.

God-is-good-all-the-time. Spin, spin, spin.

There is faith, hidden in my fingers.

Appassionato

I have autism, so I lack empathy.

That's what the "experts" say.

I am the expert.

I live it.

My very human heart knows your pain,

It is hurting,

Smiling,

Fighting alongside you

There is compassion, hidden in my fingers.

Incalzando

Sensory madness puts me in chaos

Light drives stakes into my skull, as

Sound penetrates the depths of my consciousness,

Compounded by sand paper to my skin, also known as your gentle hand

Upon my shoulder.

I retreat into inner peace.

The irony is that I am wholly present—

In the sensory experience.

I look unaware, but looks deceive,

Because there is connection, hidden in my fingers.

Calando

My face is crying.

Am I sad?

I'm pounding my forehead with my fist.

Does my head hurt?

If I don't have a keyboard,

How can I know?

But there is ability, hidden in my fingers.

Legato

Though my voice

Does not have the words

To strike up a conversation,

My fingers hide friendship.

Though my ears

Do not always hear,

So that I can make sense of the world,

My fingers listen so that I can understand.

Though my eyes dart back and forth

Rarely pausing to meet yours,

My fingers can see within,

And know a person's heart.

Though I might never

Ask you how you're doing today,

If you type to me,

My fingers will join you

In both the good and the bad.

Though you would not expect,

From such a quiet girl,

The hope and dreams

To change the world

I will do just that,

From behind my keyboard.

Timothy O'Keefe on Employment
Timothy C. O'Keefe

Presentation

Lafollette Post Grad program get me my job. I try things that I like and that I not like. I learned that I like recycling. I like the out of doors. I like the earth. I work to keep it nice.

I work M-F, 11 - 2. I shred secrets for the Madison Public Schools. They include Payroll records, grades, IEPs, and human resources records. ICW helps me keep my job. My job coaches are awesome.

My mom say "Don't tell" I say "Who I tell, I not talk."

In the nice weather before work, I volunteer with the Parks Pride Program to clean up my favorite neighborhood park, Ahuska Park in Monona. My mom teach us to give back when we were little.My sister is on the school board in Cudahy. I clean up after Little League games. We both make the world a better place.

Advice About Jobs

Jobs are for grown ups, not kids. I have behaviors, but I learn I need to knock that shit off if I want to keep my job. I am far from perfect, but I have many people who help me to get to where I want to go.

I was four when I started typing. I mostly type with my family and at meetings. I think it helps in meetings. They listen. They think differently. Even if they not sure, they not treat me like an idiot.

When I type, either they believe me or they think my mom is nuts.

It's ok for me either way.

I not seem like a guy who has a community job and a girlfriend and a paycheck. You can find meaningful paid or volunteer work if you work hard at it.

[Presentation to the Autism Society of Wisconsin
Friday April 25, 2014]

TO THOSE
Emma Zurcher-Long

The day I wrote what I could not expect my mouth to say,

was the day everything began to change.

It started as snail-like.

Not even a crawl,

more like lunging

at a moving and changing target.

Memory shouts frustration and gratitude.

I worry the found words will be lost.

Repeating sounds calm,
And now,
the words and memories dance.

I type loudly,
I am still not sure most can hear,
but words torment me less now.

This world is full of talkers.
Listening is an entry, but without the ability to talk too,
listening walks alone.

Typed words frozen on a page
silently wait to be read.

Typing gifts me with serious flames
igniting silent thoughts
now lit in glowing, neon bright, poster paint that confuses some,
but others radiate hope and ecstatic enthusiasm.

It is to those
my words twirl and spin for.

To Be Included

Tracy Thresher

To be included and respected as a contributing member in my community is exhilarating. I wonder why being included is often described as a prideful privilege by me and others. Being valued as a person is not something that requires proving worth but the reality of society is prevailing notions are what you see is the whole story.

Let me take you along my walking through chaos to come to a place of personal growth and finding my value. You must understand that love is what I longed for in the attitudes of my teachers in my school days. This is valuing me by mightily looking past my kooky behavior to expose my true intelligence.

Pushing through madness is typing therapy in my early days of sorting out anger for many lost opportunities. Mired in self-doubt with looping recall of name calling in my head I lacked the confidence but high expectations and belief in me from Alan Kurtz freed me. Passing the torch to my long-time friend Harvey Lavoy is a pivotal point in my self-discovery. I was going through big time life changing decisions. Harvey showed his commitment to me by sticking by me when my anxiety took over. To hear Harvey ask about my goals and dreams gave me a boost of hope. To have hope flickering is marvelous shot of delightful promise. Promise of commitment to fulfilling my dreams is the gift I gave to myself by working through all of the daggers of labeling that slashed at my hope and confidence.

I discovered self-advocacy. Green Mountain Self Advocates was a learning opportunity and joyfully I began to make connections with others. I began to fan my flame of hope to mentor students. With Harvey's support I began to mentor kids who also typed to communicate. I found my passion is being a mentor to kids. Being a good listener and encouraging others who have similar struggles has given my life so much purpose. Although I have many obstacles in my life I now positively find hope in the humanity of people I have met in my travels. I love educating others about the presumption of competence. My dear friend Doug Biklen is a pioneer in the United States. Pioneering Rosie Crossley has given hope to many people by leading them out of darkness and isolation through typing. As my dreams of teaching have given my life purpose I now have the opportunity to mentor others who type to communicate. Paying it forward is my big time giving hope to people who are feeling trapped by lack of communication.

Trains And Taxis
Hope Block

Trains

I love the train, but not the stations. They
are difficult for people with disabilities.
You need a Redcap to help and must avoid
escalators when your mother is with you and
isn't in good shape.

Taxis in NYC

They are crazy drivers in New York and
many don't speak good English, but they
are necessary in the city. You need every
address before you get in. Overlook their
inability to take the best road each time.

Yardsticks
Lydia Wayman

You hold me up to yardsticks as I grow,
Not marked by feet and inches but skills.
First words by two? We check it off the list.
Oh, heck; I read by two, but you don't care.
You'd diagnose that too, if you knew.

My autistic neurology is not
A purse I grab and throw over my shoulder,
And set down when it gets to be too much.
You can't remove the flour from a cake,
Once baked, each grain becomes forever a part

Deficit, impairment, lacking, symptoms.
Why all the gnashing teeth and gnarly bombs?
It's no wonder the word itself has caused
More moms to gasp for breath than uphill sprints.
Give me a smile, a keyboard, and a chance.

You want me to aim only for normalcy.
Depending on which yardstick you hold up,
Watch yourself, I might blow its top right off.
But you're stuck on measuring typicality.
I don't want to measure up to that.

Author's Note: This poem focuses on the attitude toward autism, but the "yardsticks" we are measured against often involve our spoken voices. When we are finally offered a keyboard, we display intelligence that no one expected... all because they held up the wrong measuring stick.

❖ ❖ ❖

I Don't Want Your "Protection"

Amy Sequenzia

This is for the people I refer to as "the FC police", or as someone once said, "the sheriffs".

I don't want you coming to my life to "make sure" the words I type are mine, or that my facilitators are "honest". You can't because you don't know me, or my journey. All you say only shows how incompetent you believe I am, how helpless and without determination you think I am.

It also sounds self-righteous and bullish, your stories and studies from long ago that prove nothing, that don't have anything to do with my life, my difficulties, my accomplishments and my voice.

So, come down from the pedestal you built for yourself and back off. I am going to live my life despite your assumptions of my complete detachment of what I understand to be a human being experience: full of ups and downs, trial and errors, lots of hard work and ultimately growth.

Good bye.

Now that the bullies have hopefully left, I want to talk about some important things. The title of this article still applies, especially if you presume competence.

I want to talk about "influence". This is the main concern surrounding FC and oddly enough, RPM (Rapid Prompting Method)—the assurance that our fingers are not being guided, that the words we type are really ours.

I will begin with the "guiding" issue.

It seems obvious to me that some people (I don't call them facilitators) are unscrupulous (so are some in Congress, in the banks, in the justice system, in the planet). It is also true that FC is not for everyone, which is not the same as saying that people who cannot communicate in a way easily understood by the majority are incompetent.

The skeptics and the bullies have many theories that support their continuous bullying:

The user is being guided

The facilitator unconsciously guide the user's hand (never mind that every real facilitator knows how to be aware of this "possibility", and that it is impossible to guide someone's hand by touching their shoulder, for example)

Now the "experts" that never talked to a non-speaking who types to communicate are also saying that RPM users are not the author's of their words, even though there is no physical contact whatsoever.

The bullies want to sound less bullish and now they use the code word "influence". The claim is: the simple presence of a speaking person next to us can make us type what they want us to type.

Influence is code word for: non-speaking Autistics are not competent and never will be, so the words they type are never theirs, even if nobody is touching them; they are so incompetent, anyone can influence what they say; they can never grow and learn to use their own voices.

This is discrimination. If influence is so powerful, that should be true for speaking people too. How do I know that the words coming out of my speaking friends' mouths is not being influenced by someone else? But I am not presumed to be competent, while speaking people are.

Influence is real, as we all influence each other all the time. My experience is, as I grow and mature, as I learn more about things, through reading and relationships, I am influenced by my relationships with people and with my surroundings. To me this is life, a natural part of being out in the world.

As for my typing, I am now in a safe place with my main facilitator. I am also safe with other facilitators I know and I am training someone who I trust. Besides, I have friends who will voice their concerns if they notice something odd in my typing. These are friends I trust, not self-proclaimed "defenders of honest practices". I also understand that there are expectations about what I should/will say and this might influence what I type. My feeling safe means I can reject such influences and type my mind out. I cannot control what others expect from me, but I can choose to fulfill that expectation by saying what they "want" to hear, or I can choose to say whatever I want, even if I disappoint them. My responsibility, my decision.

Who is to say that my facilitator is influencing me to the point of choosing the letters I type? If one could see our day-to-day interactions, one would understand why it is safe for me to type whatever I want. We, as human beings, have a very human relationship.

Besides, we influence each other all the time and I can argue that I exert great influence on how she says things. I am, after all, competent enough to teach her a few things. Still, it is her voice, her words.

I also want to say that I wish some people would stop idolizing typists. I am not an angel, I don't have wings and I don't ride a unicorn. Despite of my friend K. saying that I am an "actual perfect human being", she also knows I am capable of being not so nice and that I should be held accountable for whatever I type. If I am mean or if I type something hurtful, these words are still mine. No "influence" excuses. Still my responsibility.

Presume my competence because I am a human being interacting with other human beings, I grow up, learn and change. I influence and receive influence all the time. There is not a "super influence force" acting on me when I type, with or without physical contact.

Saying that typists are more easily influenced than speaking people is discriminatory and assumes that non-speaking people are incompetent, oblivious and not capable of growing to exercise self-determination. It assumes we will always need to be protected against the "superior" speaking people. I don't want this "protection".

Saying that typists are always wise and right, that everything we say is full of deep insights that only "trapped" souls can have is assuming we are more than humans. Saying that we can never hurt someone's feelings, or use words considered "bad", is also trying to paint us as angelic creatures. One cannot be presumed to be competent if one is so special and flawless. I don't want this "protection" either.

I am just a human being, living a human life. The protection I want is the protection of my right to use my voice, the way I choose to.

If you cannot live with that, shut up and back off!

❖ ❖ ❖

Contributors

Aaron Greenwood

Hello my name is Aaron Greenwood and I am 17 years old. I live in Rocky Mountain House, Alberta, Canada on my family's farm. I am in grade 11. Understand that this is a great joy to be a part of this project

Aleph Altman-Mills

Aleph Altman-Mills is an autistic poet. She blogs and posts writing prompts at darlingghosts.tumblr.com.

Alex Kimmel

Alex Kimmel is an experienced speaker. He has presented at the local, state and national levels on such key issues as Inclusion, Disability Acceptance, Culture of Gentleness and Self Determination.

He has educated and inspired students, teachers, professionals, congregations and the community at large since 2006.

Alyssa Hillary

Alyssa Hillary is an Autistic graduate student, teaching assistant, and disability studies scholar. She blogs at yesthattoo.blogspot.com and enjoys writing fiction and poetry.

Amy Sequenzia

Amy Sequenzia is a multiply Disabled, non-speaking Autistic activist and writer. She is also one of the organizers of the grassroots movement Boycott Autism Speaks. She blogs for Ollibean and Autism Women's Network, is part of the Board member of the Autism National Committee (AutCom) and the Autistic Self Advocacy Network (ASAN). Her work can be found on her blog nonspeakingautisticspeaking.blogspot.com

Astrid van Woerkom

Astrid van Woerkom is a mostly speaking autistic and blind person who was born in 1986. She is married. Astrid completed high school in 2005 and has taken various courses in psychology since. She currently lives in a residential care facility in the Netherlands. She blogs at Bloggingastrid.com.

autismdoggirl

I am a 27 year-old Autistic female and service dog handler who speaks out for autism service dog reform. I am a self advocate and college student, I spoke late but eventually gained speech, however over time I became aware being verbal came at a great cost for me and not being able to use it effectively I have gone since back to being nonspeaking and I am now a full time AAC user

Brayden Fronk

My name is Brayden Fronk. I am goofy in a good way. My family wonders about me. My age is 14. I don't talk, but I spell with a stencil. My family is good to me.

Bridget Allen

Bridget Allen is an autistic writer and activist from North Texas and founder of The Octans Partnership.

Ms. Allen writes highly personal stories of disability's intersection with poverty, feminism, queer culture, and abuse. Her work has been featured on NeuroQueer.com, the Huffington Post, and her personal blog, ItsBridgetsWord.com.

A self described "perpetual parent", Ms. Allen has been raising children with varied and complex needs for over thirty years. She currently juggles homeschooling her two youngest children, a love for vegan cooking and baking, and visits from her grandchildren

Christopher Finnes

Christopher Finnes , aged 15 , Has autism and is non-verbal, uses Rapid Prompting Method and is able to independently point to a laminated letterboard.

Chris lives in Sutton Coldfield, United Kingdom.

Christy Oslund

Christy Oslund—worked as a nanny, bookstore manager, and sheep wrangler before returning to college as a mature student. She has studied conservation, theology, philosophy, and communication and holds degrees including an MFA and PhD. Her current publications include *Supporting*

College and University Students with Invisible Disabilities: A Guide for Faculty and Staff.

Cindi Hoyal

Cindi Hoyal is a non-speaking autistic who likes to spell to communicate. She is thirteen years old and loves her family in Utah.

Conor McSorley

Conor is 7 years old and lives in Rugby, Warwickshire, UK, with his Mum, Dad and two younger sisters. He is easygoing with a very cheeky sense of humour. Apart from 'doing his words', he loves jigsaws, Lego and having a wrestle! Although Conor's speech is limited, he usually manages to make his needs known!

He has been a great inspiration to his Mum, who 5 years ago set up a successful Autism support group and now a charity!

Cori Frazer

Cori is a 23 year-old autistic person living in Pittsburgh, PA with her dog and partner.

Cynthia Kim

Cynthia Kim is the author of two books, *"Nerdy, Shy and Socially Inappropriate"* and *"I Think I Might be Autistic"*. She blogs about her experiences as a late-diagnosed woman, wife and mother at musingsofanaspie.com.

Daniel McConnell

Daniel McConnell began typing to communicate in 2007 at age 23. He completed his GED in December 2013 and attends classes at University of Wisconsin at LaCrosse. He wants to be a writer and advocate for others like himself. One of Daniel's main goals is to one day type independently. His story appears in *Real People, Regular Lives: Autism, Communication and Quality of Life* by Sally R. Young, Ph.D.

Elizabeth J. (Ibby) Grace

Ibby Grace is an Autistic professor who blogs at tinygracenotes.blogspot.com and is an editor on *i.e.: inquiry in education* (digitalcommons.nl.edu/ie/) and *NeuroQueer* (neuroqueer.blogspot.com). Her writing can also be found among other places in the books *Loud Hands, Both Sides of the Table: Autoethnographies of Educators Learning and Teaching With/In [Dis]ability,* and *Criptiques.* Ibby currently serves on the boards of Society for Disability Studies and AutCom.

Emma Charlotte Studer

For 18 years Emma Charlotte Studer watched and listened while others assumed she could not understand. In September 2010, emma began to write on paper and then type with assistance. She broke out of the self-contained classroom to graduate with a regular high school diploma. Now, at 22,she is currently attending her local college. She is assisted by her mother and other aides in her studies, as approved by accommodations. Her blog is Emmasmiraclemusic.blogspot.com

Emma Zurcher-Long

Emma Zurcher-Long was born in 2002. She is a public speaker, a writer and is Autistic. Emma cannot have a conversation with spoken words. Emma communicates by typing and wishes people would "listen to my writing voice, but they listen to my talking voice instead."

Emma's writing has been published on her blog, Emma's Hope Book, *Special Parent Magazine* and HALO's 2014 edition of *Voices.* Emma has given presentations at Autism and Disability Conferences and schools around the country.

Ethan

I am the Ethan of Provo. I am so good, kind, and mad. My good teacher is my RPM teachers. I am twelve and young. My family is nice to me.

Eva Sweeney

Eva Sweeney is a 31 year-old genderqueer disabled female who works primarily as a freelance writer. Her topics include disabilities and sex, gender and lesbian culture. She is also the creator of a documentary called "Respect: The Joy of Aides". She currently lives in LA with her two dogs

Graciela Lotharius

Graciela is an eleven year-old girl who loves expressing her new found "voice" through her laminated letter board. She is constantly trying to advocate for other "late talkers" like her and keeps encouraging her mom to "educate others about outstanding RPM". She loves her family and just about anything that goes fast—especially the big swings at the fair and her grandparents' boats. Graciela's gifts are many. She is ready to share them with the world.

Henry Frost

advocate. student. communicator. friend. #istandwithhenry

Hope Block

Hope Block is a board member of the Autism National Committee. She has presented at numerous conferences including regional and national TASH conferences, Rhode Island's Annual State-wide Self Advocacy conference, and the Society for Disability Studies. She lives in Newport Rhode Island

Jake Hunt

Hunt is a hopeful boy from American Fork. I can say quite a lot about life. I'm happy going, kind like, and funny

Joey Lowestein

Joey is 19 years old and types using the method RPM (Rapid Prompt Method)

Justin Benjamin

Justin Benjamin has Autism and communicated this message through Rapid Prompt Method (RPM) where Justin points to letters on a letter board or types them.
He has limited speech.
Age 21 years old

Kassiane A. Sibley

Kassiane Sibley is a vintage 1982 Autistic, diagnosed in 1986. She has been doing Autistic activism since 1999 or so & currently blogs at Radical Neurodivergence Speaking & We Are Like Your Child. Kassiane currently is attending university with every intention of dragging the neuroscience community kicking & screaming into the neurodiversity paradigm, and has 2 seizure detecting cats named after things found in the brain.

Kayla Miki Takeuchi

I am a person who types because I am non-verbal and autistic. My name is Kayla Takeuchi and I have been typing for seven years. In that time I have earned my high school diploma and am now in college.

Kimberly R. Dixon

Kimberly Dixon is a 29-year-old published poet from Round Rock, Texas. Kimberly has nonverbal autism, but communicates via typing. She enjoys writing, painting, riding horses, gardening, and starting conversations about intriguing topics like dreams and religion. She also enjoys collecting figurines and birdhouses. Her goal is to write poetry as a career. She hopes to use her poetry and art to make greeting cards in the near future.

In February 2014, Kimberly was recognized by the Round Rock City Council for her work as an author and artist. February 27, 2014 was proclaimed "Kimberly Dixon Day" in the City of Round Rock.

Kimberly recently published a book of her poetry and art called "*Under the Silence is Me—How It Feels to Be Nonverbal.*" The book and prints of five of her original art pieces can be purchased online at www.kimsgifts.etsy.com.

Lateef McLeod

Lateef McLeod is a spoken word artist and a poet with cerebral palsy who published his first poetry book entitled *A Declaration Of A Body Of Love* in 2010. He currently is writing a novel tentatively entitled *The Third Eye Is Crying.* More of his writings are available on his website Lateefhmcleod.com and his Huffington Post blog, http://www.huffingtonpost.com/lateef-mcleod/. He is the President-elect for the United States Society for Augmentative and Alternative Communication (USSAAC).

Leonard Schwartz

Lenny Schwartz is turning 46 years old and communicates using a letter board. He began with Soma Mukhopadhyay in May of 2008

Lily

Lily is six years old and types to communicate

Lucy Blackman

Lucy Blackman was born in Melbourne, Australia in 1972 and is an autistic poet and writer. Lucy is predominantly non-speaking and communicates by typing, movement, gesture and occasional verbalisation. In 1987 Lucy became a client of DEAL (now the Anne McDonald Centre) in Melbourne, entered mainstream education and graduated MA (Literary Studies) from Deakin University in 2005.

Her autobiography *Lucy's Story* was published both in Australia and the UK, and she is a contributor to both Douglas Biklen's *Autism and the Myth of the Person Alone* as well as to the collections of the Brisbane FC poetry group "Brotherhood of the Wordless". Lucy has presented in Australia and overseas in part to demonstrate how effective keyboards can be for people in her situation.

Recently Lucy has been working on a number of essays about language, communication and AAC. These draw on her attempts to integrate her various communication strategies with practical skills as a form of language exercise. These writings are available for comment in draft form on www.smashwords.com.

Lydia Wayman

Lydia Wayman is an autistic advocate from the Pittsburgh area. She has her B.S. in Elementary Education from Grove City College and will finish her Master's in English and Creative Writing in November, 2014. She is the author of several books about autism, an active writer in national and international publications, and a passionate speaker. Lydia is employed at Parents in Toto, an autism nonprofit that serves diagnosed individuals and their families, and she serves as the Young Adult Advisor to their Board of Directors. She is a Young Leader with the Autistic Global Initiative. She loves cats, language, and any chance for creativity. Lydia combines mostly speaking with sometimes typing into a reliable, comfortable system of communication.

Mandy Klein

I'm an autistic woman married to an autistic man and we have an autistic daughter. I am both speaking and non-speaking, sometimes typing to communicate on both computer and phone. I started my advocacy journey about two years ago and am now slowly becoming an activist. I am a doodler, I love drawing circles, and I am a para equestrian.

Mark Utter

Mark Utter is a native Vermonter who has a form of autism and types to communicate. When Mark was first introduced to a form of alternative communication called "supported typing" he found it tedious and did not see much use for it. One day Emily asked him if he would consider using supported typing with her to write some lines for the play, "I'll Fly Away."

Through this experience Mark found that he could use Supported Typing to share his story and asked Emily to support these efforts. What was intended to be a play blossomed into the film "I am in here; a view of my daily life with good suggestions for improvement from my intelligent mind." Mark has shown his movie 30 times and conducted inspirational conversations with audience members after each screening. Mark has also facilitated several workshops, has started a blog and has a new writing project in the works.

Mekhi T. Schokley

M. Shockley. He is a 11 year old, intelligent, beautiful young man. Mekhi uses a stencil board to communicate

Michael Lee

Michael Lee is a 12 year old boy with Autism, cerebral palsy, epilepsy and many other medical conditions. He is considered "not functionally verbal" even though he has many words. Most of his speech is incredibly slurred and muddled due to the extreme low tone in his mouth (most likely from his CP) and so only his family and close friends really understand speech. Frequently even they struggle and this frustrates him. They discovered RPM a little over a year ago and introduced it to him through his teacher Lenae Crandall. He has adapted to it amazingly well and has been able to show incredible depths of intelligence that previously were locked inside of him. Due to this and his special ed program at school being inflexible about researching and using RPM with Michael, he is now homeschooled using RPM exclusively. This is undoubtedly the best decision we have ever made with his input in regard to his education and future.

Michael Scott Monje, Jr.

Michael Scott Monje, Jr. is a West Michigan writer whose work centers neurodivergent and LGBT characters. They write the Shaping Clay blog, which publishes a web serial featuring an autistic child growing up in the late 1980s and early 1990s. They are also the author of three novels: the self-published *Nothing is Right* and *Mirror Project*, and *Defiant*, which is available from Autonomous Press. They also wrote the electronic chapbook *A Waking Narrative*.

Nathan Trainor

My name is Nathan Trainor and I am 30 years old. I am non-verbal and physically disabled from Jouberts Syndrome. I live in my own home in

Waverly, Iowa. I work at the recreation center at Wartburg College. I also volunteer in my community. I advocate for people with disabilities and for Facilitated Communication.

P. Allen

Musician, Digital Artist and Poet who believes that thru expression we can create understanding.
Likes Art, Music, Nature, Walking and appreciates quietness

Paul Hope Park

Paul is 23 years old autistic young man with very limited speaking ability, very smart and insightful, loves speedskating, skiiing, and playing ice hockey. He has completed 8 short version of triathlons so far. He overjoys a newly joined bowling league. Most of all, he gives me joy with such a large warm heart.

Paula C. Durbin-Westby

Paula C. Durbin-Westby is an autistic and disability rights activist. Paula is a partially speaking Autistic, or a "nonspeaking (at times)" Autistic. She is interested in learning about, promoting, and creating acceptance for methods and forms of both non-language and language-based learning and communication that are not "typical" but that are helpful for some Autistics. Paula is the founder of Autism Acceptance Day and Month, a celebration in April that counters negative messages about autism during that month. She also is developer of the Tool Kit of Resources from the Autistic Community.
http://paulacdurbinwestbyautisticblog.blogspot.com/
http://tool-kit-autistic-alternative.blogspot.com/
http://autismacceptanceday.blogspot.com/

Philip Reyes

Philip is a 6th grader at Heim Middle School in Getzville, NY where he is supported by his teachers to use a letterboard and iPad to participate in his classes. Philip is non-speaking and at age 9, first learned to communicate with a letterboard stencil from Soma Mukhopadhyay at her HALO clinic in Austin, TX. He is refining his skills to include typing on an iPad and even some speech. Philip's interests and hobbies include swimming, soccer, reading biographies, and expressing his views on his blog at www.faithhopeloveautism.blogspot.com

Quinn Partridge

Quinn Partridge graduated from high school when he was 18 and has been taking classes at the local community college. He is a valued member of his church, faith club, dance club and German club. He has had various part time jobs and is currently working on starting his own business.

Quinn enjoyed an inclusive education and is enjoying an inclusive life. Whenever possible, Quinn travels, goes biking on his recumbent bike, and is outside in nature. Mostly Quinn loves going to movies and festivals with friends. In recent years, Quinn hosted a series of cooking classes at his house. He has done national presentations on communication, self determination and the importance of community.

Last year, Quinn and his Jack Russell, Winny, moved into their own home.

Rick Maives

Rick is a 34 year old man with autism and down syndrome. He uses facilitated communication as his primary means of communication. In recent years, he has begun to mentor other FC users. He loves it and believes it is his calling to advocate for himself and others. He enjoys art as a way to express himself. He usually uses acrylic medium to create his abstract art. His work, Colors In Dream, was selected for the program cover of the Rochester Philharmonic Orchestra February 2014 bravo series. He lives in Cicero NY with his family.

Ron Giri

Ron is 9 years old; non-verbal and autistic. He uses RPM for communication either through typing in IPAD or pointing on a letter board. He lives in UK

Roy Bedward

I am Roy Bedward. I was born with a thing called autism. I have been typing for many years but never every day. I only type a couple of times a week. I am an artist. I have my own business. I sell my paintings and books. I also give presentations. When I am painting I feel more normal and happy than any other time in my life. I love color. It can make me so much more alive when I have it in my life. I'm not sure if you will understand that but it is very real for me.

Sagarika Vaidya

Sparrow Rose Jones

Sparrow Rose Jones is an Autistic author, artist and musician who is sometimes speaking and sometimes not-speaking. Sparrow lives with Fermat the cat and blogs under the name Unstrange Mind. You can find a portfolio page of Sparrow's creative work at www.sparrowrose.com.

Stephanie

I'm a usually verbal autistic adult who uses AAC to supplement speech when its lost, especially during sensory overload and migraines. I've found my place in the world helping other autistic people and using my special interest simultaneously, tutoring autistic students in math in local schools. I also hate writing biographies despite frequently writing about my autism in order to educate those around me.

Stephanie H.

Timothy O'Keefe

Timothy O'Keefe is a 27 year old young man living in Madison, Wisconsin. He graduated Lafollette High School Post Grad Program in 2009 and currently works for the Madison Public Schools Building Services. He enjoys all kinds of artistic activities, playing basketball, going to movies, listening to audiobooks (he loves Sue Grafton's Kinsey Milhone series) and watching *"Pawn Stars."* He likes to spend time with his family and his staff as well as his girlfriend

Tracy Thresher

Tracy Thresher is a native Vermonter who lives and works in Vermont. Tracy began using Facilitated Communication in 1990 and was one of the first individuals with autism in Vermont to be introduced to it. He has presented at local, statewide, national and international workshops and conferences. He has consulted with local schools and also mentors high school students, is a member of the Vermont Communication Task Force, the WCMHS Communication Alliance and does freelance work for Green Mountain Self-Advocates and works with the Institute on Communication and Inclusion at Syracuse University as a Master Trainer. Tracy and his friend, Larry Bissonnette, travel promoting their documentary *"Wretches & Jabberers"* in an effort to change the World's view of disability to one of positivity.

Email: rightsrus@wcmhs.org

Blog: www.wretchesandjabberers.org/tracy

Appendix
Elizabeth J. Grace

I Was A Self-Loathing FC Skeptic[1]

You can read in *Loud Hands: Autistic People, Speaking* about the shall-remain-nameless professor who said in front of me and many others in graduate school that autistics did not know what it was like to be themselves because they had no theory of mind, so one had to read research about them done by others in order to understand them at all, (which presumably if you were one of them, you never could anyway—this part is logically editorialized by me).

There was another professor who said in a large class of aspiring special education and psychology researchers, "Except for Grace, the idiot savant, who doesn't count," because I recalled more than seven allegedly random numbers which were not actually random, but had a clear pattern, and he hadn't told me ahead of time that the object of the exercise was to demonstrate that nobody can recall more than seven random things in short term memory.

Those two professors I mostly steered clear of. A third one, I trusted, because he seemed lovely. He told me that facilitated communication (FC) was a dangerous non-scientific fad which co-opted people's voice and autonomy, and we, as scientist-practitioners, had to reject such nonsense, even though we should still go to TASH, where some people believed in silly things. He acted as if he meant this nobly, and so I believed him. But I still didn't quite feel safe enough to tell him who I was, that his colleague had hit the nail on the head with the completely inappropriate joke of "idiot savant."

My graduate university is famous for its brilliant education program, which runs several of its own conferences, and from which one can get a job even in an economic downturn. I was well-trained in several kinds of sciencey goodness by some seriously important people. I kept my hands in my pockets all the time and made sure nobody ever came to my apartment while making a big giant show of becoming elected President of the student association to demonstrate my ever-loving sociable respectability.

I spent almost all my spoons, and became quite ill in the process, but at least I learned really important scientific academic things, like how to be patriarchally condescending toward my fellow Autistics, "protecting" them from themselves while I secretly cowered in the migraine-inducing limelight, doing whatever I could to avoid exposing my need for shade and quiet and peace. (I also learned really amazing actually useful things, such as see link

---

1. First published at tinygracenotes.blogspot.com in 2012.

below.)

So when you hear me now, as you will hear me now, defending people whose voices are made manifest by typing, you should know that I am not a scientific naif. Here is what happened: I met many people who communicate by typing (as I often do myself) and found out from them what their life experiences were. In epistemological terms, this is sometimes called phenomenological knowledge, or to put it more idiomatically, getting it from the horse's mouth. I consider its warrant stronger than that of many of the quasi- and experimental studies that have been used to devoice those who are non-speaking, because of the question of goodness-of-fit. In other words, I am a person who has been carefully trained to understand what various kinds of research studies are able to show and not show, and here is an excellent book[2] I was lucky enough to help edit for the top ed research organization[3] about just that topic, if you are interested in delving more deeply into it for yourself.

And it is because of this that I have changed my mind and attitudes about the breadth of communication choices of people whose way of communicating is through typing, even if they are not yet entirely independent with it. In other words, you can tell me all about FC being 'unscientific,' but know this is something I've thought about long and deeply, and I will likely answer you in graphic detail about ethnography, phenomenology, epistemology, knowledge warrant, and patriarchalist colonialism. I can do this for a very long time, because I was once like you are, if you are like I once was.

Thanks for listening.

Best,
Ib

---

2. *Handbook of Complementary Methods in Education Research (3rd Edition)*, Green, Camilli, & Elmore (Eds.), with Skukauskaite and Grace. Routledge, 2006.
3. AERA. (American Educational Research Association.)

CPSIA information can be obtained at www.ICGtesting.com
Printed in the USA
BVOW06s0152310715

410925BV00010B/131/P

9 780986 183522